AMSTERDAM

Welcome to Amsterdam

Carole Chester

Collins
Glasgow and London

Cover photographs
Pete Bennett: warehouse on the Singel (top rt)
Van Phillips: Het Lieverdje (top l.), sightseeing
boat (mid), Herengracht (btm l.),
bistro (btm rt)

Photographs
Pete Bennett, Studio B
pp. 13 (top rt), 17, 20 (rt), 23 (l.), 47 (top and btm rt), 51 (top l. and mid rt),
61 (l. and rt), 65 (top), 69 (btm), 74 (top and btm), 75 (btm)

Feature-pix
pp. 22, 77

Van Phillips
pp. 13 (l. and btm rt), 15 (l. and rt), 16 (l. and rt), 18, 20 (l.), 21, 23 (rt), 25, 27,
28, 32 (l. and rt), 47 (top and btm l., mid rt), 51 (btm l. top and btm rt), 52,
56 (l. and rt), 57 (l. and rt), 64, 65 (btm), 66-7, 68, 69 (top), 70, 71,
72 (l. and rt), 73, 75 (top), 78, 79, 80, 84 (top and btm),
85 (top and btm l. and rt), 86 (top and btm),
89 (top, inset and btm), 90, 91, 92

Illustrations
pp. 4-9 Peter Joyce
p. 54 Ted Carden

Maps
pp. 33-45 adapted by kind permission of Hallwag
from their city map series
pp. 55, 58-9, 60, 63, 64 by M. and R. Piggott
pp. 82-3 by Mike Shand

First published 1986
Copyright © Carole Chester 1986
Published by William Collins Sons and Company Limited
Printed in Great Britain

ISBN 0 00 447373 6

CONTENTS

AMSTERDAM

In the 13th century Amsterdam was no more than a small fishing village located at the confluence of the Amstel and IJ rivers. Whenever there was a strong northerly wind the water was swept up, causing serious flooding to the surrounding area, and so the fishermen built a dam across the Amstel as part of a protective wall to keep out the sea. It was from this construction, 'the dam in the Amstel', that the city took its name.

The first reference to Amsterdam was in a document of 1275 in which Floris V, Count of Holland, granted the people who lived near the dam toll-free passage on Dutch waterways. From then on the community quickly developed into an international trade centre. Goods were stored in warehouses here as ships loaded and unloaded before sailing on north or southwards, and Amsterdam became the leading intermediary port.

In 1323 Amsterdam became the legal port of entry for the beer imported from Hamburg and out of this grew the trade between Amsterdam and Hamburg and the Baltic ports. Once this trade was established, Dutch ships sailed further afield — to England, France and Flanders — and became more numerous on the Baltic than the ships of the German fleet.

Rapid economic growth saw the town increase in size. As shipping and trade developed, merchants began to need more room to handle and store the rising stock of goods. By the end of the 14th century this need led to the construction of the first canals. In 1481, as the town gained in importance, the first stone wall was built as fortification. Three towers dating from this era can still be seen in the city today: Schreierstoren (Tower of Tears), the Waag (Weigh House) and Munttoren (Mint Tower).

There was an honour for the town in 1489 when Holy Roman Emperor, Maximilian I of Austria, in thanks for the city's support in the power struggle with the French, granted the right to bear the imperial crown above its coat of arms. Although the right to bear the imperial crown was a true honour, it also had a practical effect: ships carrying it showed that they were under imperial protection.

You will, of course, see the coat of arms in many places today. It consists of a red shield with a black stripe on which there are three white St Andrew's crosses. The origin of the red shield is not known though the stripe may well represent the water on which the city is situated. The St Andrew's crosses may have derived from

the arms of the Persijn family who had many Knights Templar among its members and held possessions in Amsterdam in the 13th century. The shield bearers, two lions, were added to the coat of arms in the 16th century and the motto, meaning 'Courageous, Firm, Charitable', was granted by Queen Wilhelmina in 1947, after the war.

In the early years of the 16th century Protestantism took root in Holland at the same time as the Dutch provinces came under the rule of the Catholic king of Spain. At first the Spaniards concentrated on the persecution of the heretics at home and left the Dutch traders largely unmolested but when Philip II became king of Spain, in 1555, he pursued the heretics in the north as well. William of Orange, Count of Holland (known as William the Silent), took up the Dutch cause of Protestantism. Violence was rife throughout the land and many towns suffered the miseries of war or siege conditions. Amsterdam, however, remained loyal to Spain up until 1578 when the city finally agreed to join the cause for freedom from Spanish rule. The Treaty of Utrecht — the foundation of the later kingdom of the Netherlands — was concluded in 1579.

Prosperity was never greater than in the 16th and 17th centuries for it was just before 1600 that the Dutch sailed the route to the East Indies (now Indonesia). Trade with the East Indies became one of the main sources of income for Amsterdam and the Dutch East Indies Company, founded in 1602, remained an extremely profitable enterprise for two centuries. The Dutch West Indies Company was also founded, in 1621, trading with New Amsterdam (now New York City) as well as Brazil.

The city became the world's leading port and market place and also attracted many foreigners fleeing from religious persecution in their own countries. As more and more people arrived to benefit from the tolerance and prosperity of Amsterdam, the city began to bulge at the seams and its early canals were now extended in the shape of a horseshoe round the Amstel river. The same layout as you see today.

Portuguese Jews numbered among Amsterdam's rich bankers, and Jewish craftsmen from Germany and Poland became famous diamond cutters. The diamond industry, for which Amsterdam is so celebrated, is said to have been started in the 1570s by inhabitants of the Southern Netherlands fleeing the Spaniards. They

included several Antwerp diamond workers whose numbers were swelled by Polish and German Jews.

The 17th century was the Golden Age in Amsterdam, when the trader or businessman was king. The merchants had the money and built the splendid gabled houses that you see lining the canals today. Much of the fine 17th-century architecture remaining today owes its appearance to Flemish refugees who brought their own building ideas with them and adapted them to suit the Dutch character. The merchants patronized the arts to such an extent that there were as many painters as there were bakers. Of the artists of this period, the most famous, Rembrandt van Rijn, came to Amsterdam in 1623 as a young and hopeful apprentice. He spent 46 years here during which time he created 700 paintings, 300 etchings and 600 pen and ink sketches, many of which are displayed in Amsterdam's museums and galleries.

This was the time when, as an expression of civic pride, Amsterdammers wanted to build an exceptional town hall (which was later to become the Royal Palace). Work on this superb building, designed by Jacob van Campen, began in 1648 and was completed in 1655. It was so impressive that the ordinary people of the time took every opportunity to visit it. French revolutionary troops occupied Amsterdam in 1795 and, under French rule, Napoleon installed his younger brother, Louis Bonaparte, as King of Holland. He chose the town hall for his palace (1808) and some of his splendid furniture is still on view there. French rule was brief and Louis fled the capital in 1810. The return of the House of Orange (1813) gave the building back to the city and the city then gave it on loan to the royal house. In the 1930s the state finally took over ownership of the palace for the sum of ten million guilders — practically the same price as it had cost to build back in the Golden Age.

The Golden Age ended in the 18th century when English and French politicians passed laws preventing their own merchants from using Dutch ships, thus effectively breaking Amsterdam's trading monopoly. Holland declined in political and commercial importance, and there followed a period of low morale in Dutch history when industry and development flagged. The century ended in French rule but, in 1813, as Napoleon's fortunes began to wane, the Dutch people recalled the House of Orange (exiled in England) to

fill the role of king. Prince William of Orange was proclaimed the country's first king.

The 19th century was a time of steady domestic progress and it was during this period that the basis of the Netherlands' social welfare system was laid down. The arts and crafts continued to thrive and, although the great 19th-century painter, Vincent van Gogh, left his native land for France, his work has always been honoured at home and can be seen in abundance in Amsterdam's museum named after him.

The Netherlands remained neutral during the First World War. The Second World War brought misery and ruin. Despite protests of neutrality, German forces entered and occupied the country from 1940 to 1945. The working population of Amsterdam mounted a heroic strike in 1941 in protest against the deportation of Jews from the city. Strikers were arrested and shot and, within a few days, the strike had been suppressed. But it was the only time that the population of a city in occupied Europe went on strike in solidarity with their Jewish fellow citizens. Tragically, of more than 80,000 Jewish Amsterdammers, almost 70,000 died in concentration camps. One of those who

did not survive was Anne Frank whose diary of a secret life under the occupation has moved the hearts of people the world over. The house where she and her family hid from 1942 to 1944 is at Prinsengracht 263. Liberation at the hands of the Allied forces came in 1945 and the devastation of war brought determination in the Dutch people to work towards recovery.

With government and overseas aid the diamond industry soon climbed back on its feet and, three years after liberation, exports exceeded imports by nearly ten million guilders. A year later there was a huge comeback with an exhibition in the Diamond Exchange that drew 100,000 visitors. Today, there are some 13 diamond cutting works and 63 diamond workshops in and around the capital, employing more than 1000 people, including cutters, cleavers and polishers.

Once again Amsterdam occupies a leading position, exporting 400 million guilders' worth of diamonds each year. Larger stones are sold to dealers all over the world because of top-quality workmanship. It was here that the Cullinan diamond, the largest ever found, was split, in 1908, into nine large stones and 96 small brilliants. The 'Amsterdam Cut' has become world famous and many jewellers from other

countries come here to train. Since 1947 Amsterdam has boasted Europe's only diamond sorting school.

The Netherlands is a member of the European Economic Community (EEC) and a keen supporter of European cooperation. Amsterdam's commercial houses still enjoy a strong trading position despite international competition. Large commercial firms, agencies, buying combinations, advertising agencies, etc., are all located in Amsterdam. Some 26,000 people (ten per cent of the city's working population) are employed in the wholesale trade.

Amsterdam is a national and international centre for such tropical products as coffee and cocoa and also deals in dairy produce, textiles, timber, metals, chemicals, packaging materials and motor cars. Other products range from potatoes and wine to building materials and electrical goods.

The city is a major international financial centre. This finance sector is quite diverse: credit loans and exchange transactions, securities, stocks and shares, investments, insurance and re-insurance are all concentrated in the capital. The Amsterdam Stock Exchange, opened in 1611, is one of the oldest in the world, so it is not surprising that the number of foreign shares listed is greater than that of any other European exchange. Amsterdam, too, is the largest European exchange for American stocks. There are 34 branches of foreign banks here and around 37,000 people are employed in the financial sector.

In the city's early days, industrial development evolved from shipping, the metal industry and the processing of imported products. Over the years industry has expanded to include other areas. Most important today are the electronics industry, building, printing, clothing textile and shoe industries, chemical and, to a lesser extent, the petro-chemical industries. Research takes place on a large scale in Amsterdam in the Shell Laboratory, AKZO and the National Aviation and Space Laboratory.

The sea link is as important as ever. It was in 1824 that the North Holland Canal was opened and, in 1876, the North Sea Canal which connects Amsterdam with the sea via the locks at IJmuiden. The Amsterdam-Rhine Canal, navigable by day or night, connects the city with the heart of Europe, providing easy passage from the Dutch capital to the Ruhr, and vice versa.

Rail communications are excellent and Netherlands Rail connects Amsterdam with all the other major cities in Europe. There is also a first-class road network.

Schiphol Airport is an increasingly important factor in the economic life of Amsterdam. Over 27,000 people are currently employed at Schiphol and 65 different airlines fly scheduled flights in and out. Airline services, including charters, operate to 170 destinations in 80 countries.

At Schiphol East (the old airport), companies such as Fokker, KLM, Martinair and Transavia, plus ancillary industries, supply aircraft parts and navigational equipment. Air transport facilities have encouraged firms to open up in the airport vicinity. Over 50 foreign companies, manufacturers of consumer goods such as electrical equipment and optical and medical instruments, use Schiphol as a distribution centre for exports to other parts of Europe and the Near East. As a freight airport, Schiphol has ranked fourth in Europe for some years. As a passenger airport, it is frequently voted the best.

Amsterdam claims to be the fourth most important tourist centre in Europe (after Paris, London and Rome), visited each year by well over two million foreigners as well as more than two million Dutch. Not all visitors come to enjoy the city's impressive architecture and amusements, many come to attend a conference or exhibition.

Both the RAI exhibition centre and international conference centre are housed under one roof, with an underground car park (the largest in the Netherlands) for 2100 cars. The present RAI was opened in 1961 and considerably expanded in subsequent years. (The RAI Association was established in 1893 for the purpose of organizing a national bicycle exhibition.)

The RAI itself fulfils an important economic role. In addition to theatrical and other cultural events held here, there are dozens of international scientific and industrial conferences. Each exhibition and trade fair involves thousands of people, generates millions of guilders and provides indirect employment for more than 2000 people. Since its opening the RAI has received 40 million visitors.

Amsterdam's future, like its past, rests on trade and commerce, one reason why this year (1985) sees the opening of the World Trade Centre, in Amsterdam South, housing companies directly or indirectly connected with international trade.

PAPERWORK

Passports A valid passport (or Visitors Card, valid for one year, for UK citizens) is all that is required of UK, US or Canadian nationals entering Holland. No visa is necessary for a stay of up to three months, and only those arriving from a known infected area (e.g., some Asian and African countries) need worry about health or vaccination certificates. Children under 16 do not require their own passport provided they are travelling with their parents or a person of the same nationality in whose passport they are entered.

UK citizens can apply for a passport at offices in London, Liverpool, Peterborough, Glasgow, Newport or Gwent; residents of Northern Ireland should apply to the Foreign and Commonwealth Passport Agency, 30 Victoria St., Belfast. US citizens can apply to the US passport agencies in Boston, Chicago, Miami, New Orleans, New York City, San Francisco or Washington. Canadian citizens can apply by mail to the Passport Office, 125 Sussex Drive, Ottawa, Ontario K1A 0G2, or, in person, at offices in Edmonton, Halifax, Montreal, Toronto, Vancouver or Winnipeg.

Insurance It cannot be recommended too strongly that you take out sufficient insurance to cover yourself in the case of sudden illness or an accident or loss of luggage or personal items. Travel companies offering package holidays feature short-term holiday insurance which covers all the main areas of risk, but be sure to read the small print. Additional coverage may well be worth while. There are many long-term insurance schemes available, often with savings if you are a credit card holder.

UK citizens have an advantage when it comes to health insurance, since both Britain and Holland are EEC members. Under a reciprocal agreement between the two governments, medical costs are substantially reduced. You do, however, need form E111 to show that you are entitled to medical benefits under the British National Health Service. To obtain this form, ask your local office of the Department of Health and Social Security for leaflet SA28, which gives full particulars of health services in all EEC countries; and fill in form CM1 on the back page.

US and Canadian citizens should ensure that their own medical insurance covers them while abroad or, alternatively, take out short-term insurance — any insurance broker or travel agent will advise.

The standard of medical care in Holland is very high and most doctors and dentists speak English.

CURRENCY

The Dutch unit of currency is the guilder, sometimes called the florin, which is divided into 100 cents. Notes are issued in denominations of $2\frac{1}{2}$, 5, 10, 25, 100 and 1000 guilders. Coins come in denominations of 1, 5, 10 and 25 cents and 1 and $2\frac{1}{2}$ guilders. Prices are shown as Dfl.

There are banks with exchange facilities for travellers' checks and bank notes throughout the city and all the large hotels will change money for you. In addition exchange offices offer a similar service, often outside of banking hours. In Amsterdam exchange offices can be found at Centraal Station (open daily, including Saturdays, 0700-2245, Sundays 0800-2245); Amsterdam-Amstel (open daily 0800-2000, Sundays 1000-1600); KLM Building, Leidseplein (open daily 0830-1730, Saturdays 1000-1400); Centraal Station, Schiphol Airport (open daily 0800-2000, Sundays 1000-1600).

Banks are open Mondays to Fridays 0900-1600, closed Saturdays, Sundays and public holidays (p. 30). American Express, Damrak 66, is open Mondays to Fridays 0900-1700 and Saturdays 0900-1200. The Change Express exchange office, at Leidsestraat 100, is open Mondays to Sundays 0800-2400. And Thomas Cook exchange office, Dam 19, is open Mondays to Fridays 0900-1700, weekends 0900-1430; and at Leidseplein 31a, from Monday to Sunday 0830-2200.

Major credit cards are accepted throughout. International arrangements exist at certain banks for the cashing of personal checks accompanied by a major credit card, for a small fee. Your own bank at home will give you details.

There are no currency restrictions for foreigners entering Holland as tourists.

CUSTOMS

There are few restrictions on what you can bring into Holland. Articles for personal use or small gifts are not dutiable and you can bring in as much money as you like. Personal items might include two cameras with a reasonable amount of film; two cine cameras; tape recorder; binoculars; typewriter; most normal camping and sports equipment.

Importing, exporting, transit or the possession in public of any weapon is naturally strictly forbidden, although there are special regulations concerning hunting weapons. It is also illegal to bring drugs into the country (unless they are medically-approved, prescribed medicines), or any animal which has not been vaccinated against rabies.

Since Britain and Holland are both EEC members, UK visitors may import a greater quantity of duty-free cigarettes, spirits, wines and perfumes than residents of non-EEC countries. That means up to 300 cigarettes or 150 cigarillos or 75 cigars or 400 gm tobacco; up to 1½ litres of spirits over 22 per cent proof or up to three litres under 22 per cent proof (i.e., fortified wines); plus up to five litres of still wines.

You are also allowed up to 75 gm perfume and 375 cc toilet water.

Complete information on customs regulations for entering Holland may be obtained from the Dutch consulate in your country of origin, and local customs authorities provide leaflets containing hints for returning residents.

The chart below summarizes what travellers may bring home free of duty. (People under 17 years of age are not entitled to tobacco and drinks allowance.)

Duty-free allowances *subject to change*		Bought duty free or outside EEC	Duty and tax paid in EEC
Tobacco	Cigarettes	200	300
	or		
	Cigars *small*	100	150
	or		
	Cigars *large*	50	75
	or		
	Pipe tobacco	250 gm	400 gm
Alcohol	Spirits *over 38.8° proof*	1 litre	1½ litres
	or		
	Fortified or sparkling wine	2 litres	3 litres
	plus		
	Table wine	2 litres	5 litres
Perfume		50 gm	75 gm
Toilet water		250 cc	375 cc
Other goods		£28	£210

Double if you live outside Europe

US customs permit duty-free $300 retail value of purchases per person, 1 quart of liquor per person over 21, and 100 cigars per person.

HOW TO GET THERE

By Air

From the UK both British Airways and KLM (the Dutch national airline) offer frequent, almost shuttle, service several times daily to Amsterdam out of London (Heathrow). BA also operates a service from Birmingham and Manchester, KLM from Glasgow and Manchester. British Caledonian offers London (Gatwick), Glasgow and Newcastle services and Air UK has services out of Aberdeen, Edinburgh, Humberside, Leeds/Bradford, Norwich, Southampton and Stansted.

British Midland Airways operates a route from the East Midlands to Amsterdam. Additionally, there are services from Cardiff-Bristol and Teesside on Dan Air, and from Belfast, Birmingham, Guernsey and Jersey on the NLM City Hopper. Aer Lingus operates from Dublin, Cork and Shannon.

Most of the airlines feature a variety of fares, including really low-priced return fares on flights which need only be booked the day prior to departure. Though the exact departure time cannot be guaranteed, savings are enormous and flight frequency is such that no real problems should arise.

From Canada there are direct flights out of Montreal and Toronto to Amsterdam on Air Canada or KLM. One of the most economical of the scheduled fares is APEX which must be purchased at least 21 days ahead of departure and also has length of stay conditions. Many charter flights operate between Canada and Holland.

From the US, KLM operates out of L.A., Chicago, New York City, Atlanta and Houston. The number of flights varies with the season. TWA also operates a direct flight out of New York City.

Airport
Schiphol International Airport is considered to be one of the finest in Europe, both in its facilities and its efficiency. It is virtually English speaking. All signs are in English as well as Dutch and the symbols used are recognized internationally. It is only a short walk to the baggage area and, from there, on to ground transport and car rental desks, bank and information counter.

Schiphol is noted for its great variety of well-stocked duty-free shops. There are facilities, too, for the disabled, a child-care room, showers, and day rooms where you can rest for a few hours.

Taxi or limousine service is available into town, but a solo traveller will save money by taking the KLM bus to any of three destinations: Centraal Station, Museumplein or the Hilton, all roughly a half hour's ride. (Airport hotels operate their own courtesy minibus service.)

By Train
A boat-train operates between Harwich and the Hook of Holland with an onward rail connection to Amsterdam. There are departures every day and sleeping accommodation and food service are available on the ferry. Arrival point in the capital is Centraal Station where there are information offices, buses, trams and taxis.

By Sea
Holland is served by frequent ferry service for passengers with or without cars from several British ports. The most important sea connections are: Harwich-Hook of Holland on Sealink, with two sailings daily. Day crossing takes 6¾ hours, night crossing about 8 hours. North Sea Ferries operates a 13-hour night crossing from Hull to Rotterdam Europoort. From Sheerness to Vlissingen (Flushing) there are two daily sailings on Olau Line. Day crossing takes 7 hours, night crossing 8½

hours. From Great Yarmouth to Scheveningen, Norfolk Line operates three daily sailings Monday-Friday plus two on Saturday, each taking about 8 hours. Townsend Thoresen features two daily sailings Monday-Friday, plus one on Saturday, between Felixstowe and Rotterdam, taking 7 to 8 hours.

Visitors can also reach Holland via Belgium: Hull to Zeebrugge (North Sea Ferries); Dover-Ostend (by Jetfoil — British Rail/Sealink/RTM); Dover-Zeebrugge (Townsend Thoresen); Felixstowe-Zeebrugge (Townsend Thoresen).

By Bus
A number of British tour operators, such as National Bus Co., Warners, Time Off, offer their own bus/ferry holidays to Amsterdam. Several bus companies sell tickets for the journey alone: Transalpino, for people under 26, by bus and train via Harwich-Hook of Holland; Grey Green Coaches via Dover-Zeebrugge; Hoverspeed UK Ltd by bus via Dover/Calais or Boulogne; The Miracle Bus Co. via Dover-Zeebrugge; Supabus via Dover-Zeebrugge.

There are usually several daily and one night departure from various points in the UK. Discounts are often offered to students and children. And these days, long-distance buses are surprisingly comfortable with a toilet on board, hot drinks, reclining seats and video entertainment.

GETTING AROUND

Amsterdam is divided into six fare zones, though the visitor will rarely travel beyond Zone 1, Centrum (centre). Public transport is very good: 16 tram lines, 30 bus lines and two metro lines operate throughout the city until midnight and after that there is a choice of eight night bus routes. City transport is run by GVB (Municipal Transport Board), telephone information (0700-2300 hours) on 27-27-27.

Strip tickets, valid on bus, tram and metro, should be purchased in advance. Fifteen strip tickets are the most economical and are available at railway stations, post offices, tobacconists, the VVV information and ticket office opposite Centraal Station, open 0700-2300 Monday to Friday, 0800-2300 weekends, or GVB offices at: Prins Hendrikkade 108-114, open Monday to Friday 0845-1645; Amstel Railway Station, open Monday to Friday 0700-2000, weekends 1015-1700. It is possible to buy six or ten strip tickets on the buses and trams but as this costs more it is better to buy in advance. Tickets

Centraal Station

VVV office (above)

include transfers to other bus, tram or metro lines.

Metro

The two metro lines run east from the centre of the city and the service operates 0600-2400. If you plan to use the metro over a period of days it will be worth your while to buy a strip ticket (see above) in advance. The day ticket allows you to travel on all metro, bus and tram lines for one day and the following night. Two-, three- and four-day tickets may only be purchased from the GVB offices (addresses above).

In every metro station there are automatic ticket machines for day tickets and for single trips covering one to three zones. The yellow machines for stamping strip tickets are sited near the stairs leading to the platforms. When you stamp your ticket always use one strip more than the number of zones you are crossing, i.e., for one zone, stamp the second strip.

There are escalators and lifts in all metro stations except for Waterlooplein. To enter or exit from a carriage just push the *deur open* button and the doors will operate automatically.

Buses

Buses operating within city limits are yellow and bear their number and destination on the front. If you with to purchase a day ticket, board from the front. This ticket will also enable you to travel on other forms of public transport at no extra cost. The yellow stamping machine for strip tickets (see above) is to the left of the front door in buses. Buses operate from 0600 to 2400.

Night Buses After midnight there is a night bus service which covers a number of routes and runs every half hour to 0200, hourly thereafter. Strip tickets plus one-, two-, three- and four-day tickets can be used on night buses on the night(s) following the day(s) on which they are valid.

Trams

Trams also operate from 0600 to 2400 and are an excellent way of getting around the city. Eleven of the 16 lines start at Centraal Station and you can get to practically anywhere you plan to go cheaply and easily. The day ticket is a very good buy — board at the front when you need to buy one. Strip tickets (see above) are stamped on board, at the rear in trams.

Inter-city Buses

Strip tickets (see above) are also valid for inter-city travel by bus. From Amsterdam, for example, buses run every half hour to Haarlem and Leiden and almost every 20 minutes to Utrecht.

Trains

The Netherlands Railway Corporation (N.S. for short) is one of Europe's most efficient systems. There are frequent departures from Amsterdam to other cities of interest, e.g., every 15 minutes to Haarlem or The Hague. For brief visits to nearby places, a day round-trip ticket is the most economical, but a one-day ticket offering unlimited travel is also available if your destination is further away. Three- and seven-day unlimited travel tickets are also offered, along with special round-trip weekend fares.

There is no need to buy first-class

tickets as Dutch trains are clean and comfortable and most journeys are short anyway.

The seven-day ticket can be purchased at any railway station in Holland, and you will need to show your passport.

There are hourly services on most lines with anything from two to eight services hourly on busy sections. Railway timetables in English can be bought from stations and information on all public transport is available from the VVV (tourist information) or GVB offices.

Taxis

Chances of hailing a taxi in the street are not very high, instead you will find them lined up in ranks near railway stations and other key points. All taxis are metered and the fare rises from a basic starting charge. Fares are rather expensive but do include a service charge, so only tip small change. Any hotel, restaurant, etc., will telephone a taxi for you but the general number to call yourself is 77-77-77 in Amsterdam.

Car Rental

Many international car rental firms have offices in Amsterdam. They charge a daily rate plus mileage or, in some cases, offer a special deal based on unlimited mileage. Credit cards are accepted in payment and, although the minimum driving age is 18, most companies will not consider renting a car to anyone under 21 (in a few cases, to anyone under 23). But, frankly, hiring a car is a waste of time and money in Amsterdam where it is so easy to get around on foot or by public transport. What's more, finding a parking space is a *big* problem.

If you do wish to rent a car, try any of the following: Avis, Keizersgracht 485, 1017 DL, tel: 26-22-01: Budget, Overtoom 121, 1054 HE, tel: 12-60-66; Diks Autoverhuur, Van Ostadestraat 278-280, 1073 TW, tel: 72-33-66; Hertz (also rents cars with driver), Overtoom 333, 1054 JM, tel:12-24-41; Kaspers En Lotte, Van Ostadestraat 232-4, 1073 TT, tel: 71-70-66; Kuperbus B.V., Middenweg 175, 1098 AM, tel: 93-87-90; Vanwijk, Prinsengracht 737, 1017 JX, tel: 23-61-23.

Motoring Organizations

Motorists who are members of the Automobile Association, the Royal Automobile Club or the Royal Scottish Automobile Club in Britain, the American Automobile Association or the Automobile Club and Touring Club of Canada, can benefit from reciprocal services offered by the Alliance Internationale du Tourisme (AIT) in Holland. The sister organization of the AA is the ANWB, Museumplein 5, tel: 73-08-44. The other automobile association is

the Royal Netherlands Automobile Club, the KNAC, Westvlietweg 118, Leidschendam, P.O. Box 446, 2260 AK, tel: (070) 99-27-20.

Rules of the Road

The Dutch drive on the right and pass on the left. Right of way is given to traffic from the right in all cases, including roundabouts. Give way to traffic from the left arriving from roads with right of way, and at major crossroads. People on pedestrian crossings have right of way as do tram passengers getting on or off. Trams and buses have right of way over everything, and do watch out for the thousands of cyclists!

Roads are classified according to the European numbering system. General maximum city speed limit is 50kph/31mph unless there is a blue sign with white lettering which reads *70 kilometer toegestaan*. Priority roads are marked with a sign showing an orange square or diamond bordered by white. Mopeds and cycles are forbidden on motorways and highways.

Bicycles Most roads include a cycle path — a separate lane indicated by a white cycle symbol painted on the road surface. Obligatory cycle paths are indicated by a round sign with a white cycle on a blue background. Optional paths are indicated by a small black oblong sign which reads *fietspad* or *rijwielpad* — these paths are for cycles but *not* mopeds.

Bicycles must not travel two abreast if that hinders other traffic, must not travel on motorways and must use effective, working lights between sunset and sunrise. Changes in direction must be clearly signalled. Maximum speed for mopeds in built-up areas is 30kph/19mph and the minimum age for riding a moped is 16.

Safety regulations require all car drivers and front-seat passengers to wear seat belts and all motorcycle, scooter and moped drivers, and passengers, to wear crash helmets. A red warning triangle should be carried by motorists in case of breakdown.

Speed limit is normally 50kph/31mph in built-up areas and 80kph/50mph outside. On highways and motorways the usual speed limit is 100kph/62.5mph. Maximum speed for trailers using motorways is 80kph/50mph, and 60kph/37.5mph on other roads outside of built-up areas. Drive slowly in residential areas where there is a sign showing a white house on a blue background (children may be playing in the street).

Lights must be dipped after sunset and during the day if weather conditions warrant. Do not use headlights when there is

Canal bike

Cycle path

sufficient street lighting, when there is oncoming traffic or when following at a short distance behind another vehicle.

Petrol *(benzine)* stations are found along most motorways and highways and they have free toilet facilities. Fuel prices are fairly standard and service stations are plentiful.

Stopping or parking is forbidden on pavements, footpaths and cycle lanes, pedestrian crossings, highways and motorways except at designated parking spots, on connecting approach lanes, too close to pedestrian crossings or bus stops and all the other usual prohibited places. **Fines** for retrieving a car that has been towed away (e.g., for parking in the wrong place) are high.

Road service, help and repairs are available from the ANWB which has yellow call boxes along many roads. If you need help, use a call box to contact the area road service in Amsterdam on 26-82-51. The ANWB's yellow road service cars *(wegenwacht)* do patrol the most important routes between 0700 and midnight, in any case, on the lookout for motorists in distress. This service is not free and you may need to become a temporary member for a small fee, after which road service will be provided free of charge.

Drinking and driving is not advisable. The legal limit for alcohol is 0.5 millilitres per litre of blood.

Accidents The police will not come to a minor accident when the two parties involved merely fill out the necessary insurance forms. In the case of a bad accident, call the police on 22-22-22 and/or the medical service on 5-55-55-55.

Bicycle Rental

Amsterdam is a city of cycles, some 550,000 of them. You can rent a bike by

the day almost anywhere, though it is considerably less if you hire by the week. Mopeds cost more but in all cases prices vary and fluctuate. The deposit can be hefty but it is refundable. The following is a brief selection from many in the city: Fiets-O-Fiets, Amsterdamse Bos, Amstelveenseweg 880-900, tel: 44-54-73; Heja, Bestevaerstraat 39, 1056 HG, tel: 12-92-11; Koenders, Utrechtsedwarsstraat 105, 1017 VK, tel: 23-46-57; Koenders Rent A Bike, Stationsplein Oostzijde (eastside), 1012 AB, tel: 24-83-91.

Bikes may also be rented at railway stations, and they can be transported by train.

Water Transport

The newest form of waterborne travel is the canal bike which holds two to four people. It is a very simple, stable pedalboat which you can use to explore the canal system in your own way, in your own time. You will be provided with a map but are free to choose your own route, and you can return the canal bike to any one of three other locations. The four locations are: on Leidseplein, between the Marriott and American hotels; between the Rijksmuseum and the Heineken Brewery; on Prinsengracht at the Westerkerk; and on the Keizersgracht near the Leidsestraat. Rental is hourly, and for further information telephone 26-55-74.

A number of companies operate guided canal sightseeing trips in glass-roofed flat-bottomed boats. Journey time averages 1½ hours, and trips take you through the major waterways past many of the main sights. The principal departure points include: Holland International, Prins Hendrikkade, tel: 22-77-88; Rederij Plas, Damrak, quays 1, 2 and 3, tel: 24-54-06; Rederij P. Kooy, Rokin near Spui, tel: 23-

38-10; Rederij de Meeren, summer departures Amsterdam-Alphen from Sloterkade 163 near Zeilbrug, tel: 071-17-01-12; Rederij Lovers, Prins Hendrikkade, opposite No. 25-27, tel: 22-21-81; Rederij Noord-Zuid, Stadhouderskade, opposite Park Hotel, tel: 79-13-70.

ACCOMMODATION

Though the Amstel is still considered *the* hotel in Amsterdam (for its grandeur and its position overlooking the Amstel river), it does not occupy the best site in terms of being within easy reach of the main shopping and nightlife areas. All accommodation in the centre, Centrum (anywhere within the boundary of the Prinsengracht), is within easy walking distance of many of the city's points of interest.

This central area is too small to split up into specific districts, though you can expect hotels on or near Dam Square and Leidseplein to be noisy, and those in or near the Jordaan, more peaceful. In addition to chain hotels, such as Hilton and Marriott, Amsterdam boasts some particularly interesting independent hotels. The Canal House, for example, is a converted 17th-century patrician mansion on the Keizersgracht, and the Ambassade, on the Herengracht, comprises five canal houses joined together. In the luxury class, the Krasnapolsky, right on Dam Square, reflects the Edwardian era, while the first-class American Hotel is a Leidseplein landmark whose façade and art-nouveau restaurant have acquired the status of protected monuments. Yet another interesting hotel is the Pulitzer, on Prinsengracht, comprising 17 canal houses built around a series of courtyards and linked by glass-enclosed walkways.

Hotel categories range from one to five stars, visible outside the hotel. Stars are awarded by the Netherlands National Tourist Office, the Royal Dutch Touring Club and the Royal Netherlands Automobile Club. An additional open star means that the hotel is distinguished in some special way. The five-star properties are luxury; the four-star, first class; the three-star, very comfortable; the two-star, comfortable; and the one-star, plain but comfortable.

Hotel prices include service and tax and, with the exception of luxury-class hotels, usually a typical, substantial Dutch breakfast besides. Some of the older, smaller establishments do offer differently rated rooms, perhaps because of size (e.g., single), or location (e.g., at the back of the house or on the top floor when there is no lift), or some may not have a private bath.

It is worth bearing in mind that the converted, canalside mansion hotel is not usually suitable for the disabled as there is generally no lift and stairs are very steep and narrow. Most of the top hotels, however, do feature facilities for the disabled. It is also worth noting that such hotels often have rooms specifically suited to the travelling woman. The Sonesta is one of the few hotels with its own garage, a point to remember as parking is one of Amsterdam's biggest problems.

There is no self-catering within the city, though a small hotel might have a kitchenette. If you are looking for the equivalent of a guest house, go for the small simple hotels known as 'hotelettes'. Although hundreds of houseboats sit on the canals, they are privately owned and, unless you know somebody, renting one for a short period of time is impossible.

As a guide only (1985 prices), expect to pay around Dfl 60-90 for a double room in

Krasnapolsky Hotel on the Dam

American Hotel on Leidseplein

a good budget hotel and up to over Dfl 400 in a luxury hotel. A full list of hotels in all categories, including guest houses, is available from any overseas Netherlands National Tourist Office or from the VVV (tourist information office) Stationsplein 10, Amsterdam. Holland does have bungalows and summer houses for rent, but they are to be found only outside the capital.

The better hotels have their own reservation offices or are represented in the UK, US and Canada. Some hotel chains are linked to airline reservation systems, e.g., Golden Tulip Hotels are linked to KLM. To book accommodation write, telephone or telex the Nederlands Reserverings Centrum (Netherlands Reservation Centre), P.O. Box 404, 2260 AK Leidschendam; tel: (070) 20-25-00; telex 33755. Do specify desired area, time, type of accommodation, number of rooms, etc., in as much detail as possible. Your reservation will be confirmed (free) in writing or by telex.

The hospitable Dutch also promise to find you a room even if you arrive without a reservation: The VVV *Logies Informatie Dienst* (Accommodation Service) is a nationwide hotel reservation system run by the tourist office, designed to find you a room the same day or during the next few days. There is a small charge for this service and you cannot phone in for a reservation. Turn up at one of the two VVV offices: Centraal Station, Stationsplein 10; or Leidseplein 15.

Babysitters may be arranged by the better hotels or you can contact Linie van Vrijwilligers, tel: 72-36-50 (between 1100 and 1500) or Babysitcentrale, tel: 23-17-08 (1730-1900).

FOOD & DRINK

For years the Dutch tourist office has been trying to persuade restaurants to agree to a 'Taste of Holland' tag on their menus, without success. Yet the funny thing is that most of the small restaurants Amsterdammers love to feature Dutch cuisine: lots of fish, ham, bacon and pork in all its varieties, thick winter soups like *erwtensoep* (pea soup), and, of course, cheese. If dishes are not exciting by international standards, they are certainly hearty.

Restaurants, cafés and bars are numerous and the city centre is so compact that you are never far from a wide range of them. Many of the bars serve hot and cold snacks, and the locals use the cafés for breakfast or lunch as well as the odd coffee or drink. A favourite meal, for example, is an *uitsmijter* (the word means 'bouncer') comprising buttered bread topped with

roast beef or ham plus a couple of fried eggs.

Snacks, any time of the day, are an Amsterdam way of life and they are available from stand-up street stalls or in sit-down coffee shops. Plain cake often comes with a hotel breakfast (along with cold meats, ham and hard-boiled eggs). In the bakeries/coffee shops you'll find pastries and fruit-filled breads (e.g., apple or banana). And *broodjes* (sandwiches) can be purchased whenever a hunger pang hits. They are soft buttered rolls with all kinds of fillings from eel or herring to cold roast beef or tuna. Look for the sign *broodjeswinkel* (sandwich shop).

The snack is herring, especially the new herring brought in at the start of the fishing season. There is a prize for the fisherman bringing in the first catch. New herring come into Amsterdam round about 1 June, though I was still trying excellent ones in July. The best, I think, are from the street stalls all over the city. The approved way to eat herring is to pick it up by the tail, hold it aloft and swallow it. However, stall holders are well used to serving it gutted, chopped and smothered with onions for a couple of guilders.

Cheese turns up in soups and soufflés, is a breakfast certainty, and is most popular in croquettes. Nor do you have to leave Amsterdam to find a cheesemaker — there's one in the Arts & Crafts Centre, Nieuwendijk 16. Pancakes are another love and come with sweet or savoury fillings. Look out for the pancake houses if you want an inexpensive meal. A plus factor is that most cafés serve *fresh* orange juice.

There is no specific area for eating out, though Leidseplein and the streets running off it have countless cafés and restaurants, and the Jordaan area is good for brown cafés (see below). Top-class restaurants are mainly found in the luxury hotels such as the Amstel or L'Europe. The Dutch, by the way, tend to dine early, generally between 6 and 8pm.

The brown café, Papeneiland

To eat on the cheap, find a day or tourist menu — the Amsterdammers say, 'eating out of the wall', which in plain terms means from an automat. A number of restaurants offer a tourist menu for a set, inclusive price, though the price itself may vary between restaurants. Other restaurants have agreed to a fixed-price, three-course tourist menu (see list below).

You will, of course, find all types of ethnic cuisine in the city, but the Indonesian *rijsttafel* (rice table) should not be missed. It ranges from simple to elaborate and consists of a large bowl of rice accompanied by anything from 12 to 50 *sambals* (side dishes), many of which are quite highly spiced. The best-known dishes are *sate* (charcoal-grilled pieces of meat on a skewer, served with peanut sauce) and *loempia* (a kind of egg roll). Most of the food is prepared with herbs and spices such as coriander, ginger, tamarind and turmeric. The reason for the proliferation and excellence of Indonesian restaurants is that the Dutch occupied the islands of Indonesia for over three centuries until 1949. After that time many Indonesians came to Holland and they are now assimilated into Dutch society.

No grapes grow in Holland which means that wine is imported and expensive, but beer, such as Pils and Heineken, is widely drunk. So is *jenever* (gin) in its *jonge* (young) form with less sugar, or *oude* (old), often served iced, or in its sweet forms: *bessenjenever* (blackcurrant) or *citroenjenever* (lemon), known to the Dutch as 'ladies' gins'.

The Brown Cafés

The *bruine kroeg* is the Dutch equivalent of an English pub and there are said to be some 500 of them in Amsterdam. These taverns, often housed in centuries-old buildings, are frequented by the Amsterdammers themselves. The 'brown' refers to the smoke-stained walls and dark brown floors, wooden tables and beams. And many a happy, convivial hour is whiled away in them. Most brown cafés serve snacks such as toasted sandwiches and the like. One of the oldest is *De Reiger*, Nieuwe Leliestraat 34, in the Jordaan district. The atmosphere's terrific and in the most popular brown cafés it is often standing room only. Among the best are: *De Sproeier*, Leliegracht, with canalside tables in summer; *De Prins*, Prinsengracht 124, near Anne Frank House; *De Eland*, Prinsengracht 296; *Papeneiland*, Prinsengracht 2, over 300 years old; *Hoppe*, Spui 18-20, built in 1670 and always jam-packed.

The Tasting Houses

These, too, are interesting pubs widely used by local business people. They welcome tourists, though they'd hate a busload to descend on them at one time. Tasting houses are traditional drinking places selling an amazing variety of liqueurs and jenevers (Dutch gin) as well as the more usual spirits. The tulip-shaped glasses used for the jenevers and liqueurs are filled right up to the brim so the first sip must be taken by bending mouth to glass, not picking up glass to mouth. A tasting house in Dutch is known as a *proeflokaal*. Best known are: *De Drie Fleschjes* (The Three Bottles), Gravenstraat 18, just behind Dam Square; standing room only — no tables. *Wijnand Fockinck*, Pijlsteeg 31, another old house; standing room only.

Tourist Menu Restaurants

All of the following offer a fixed-price, three-course meal:
Café Americain Leidseplein 97 (tel: 24-53-22).
Artis Restaurant Plantage Middenlaan 43 (tel: 22-60-87).
Ashoka Geldersekade 23 (tel: 26-66-62).
China Indian Restaurant Ling Nam Binnen Bantammerstraat 3 (tel: 26-65-79).
Restaurant Golden Chicken Rembrandtsplein 7 (tel: 26-22-46).
Coffeeshop Haesje Claes Nieuwe Zijds Voorburgwal 320 (tel: 24-99-98).
H.R. De La Haye Leidsegracht 114 (tel: 24-40-44).
C.R. Heineken Hoek Kleine Gartmanplantsoen 1-3 (tel: 23-07-00).
Restaurant Iboya Korte Leidsedwarsstraat 29 (tel: 15-01-95).
Museum Hotel P.C. Hooftstraat 2 (tel: 71-21-03).

Norway Inn Kalverstraat 65-69 (tel: 26-23-26).

Restaurant Oud Holland Nieuwe Zijds Voorburgwal 105 (tel: 24-68-48).

Restaurant De Roode Leeuw Damrak 93 (tel: 24-96-83).

Sonesta Hotel Kattengat 1 (tel: 21-22-23).

Restaurant De Verguide Lantaarn Nieuwendijk 145 (tel: 24-54-13).

Restaurant Wienerwald Kalverstraat 180 (tel: 23-76-93).

Top-Class Restaurants

The following are among the best-known Amsterdam eating places offering Dutch cuisine, but they are expensive.

Dikker & Thijs Prinsengracht 444 (tel: 26-77-21). A classic place to dine in the grand manner. Dinner only. Closed Sundays. (Under the same ownership, *Prinsenkelder*, downstairs, is less formal and open for lunch and dinner Monday to Saturday.)

D'Vijff Vlieghen (Five Flies), Spuistraat 294 (tel: 24-83-69), is famous for its decor more than anything else. Five lopsided houses, dating from 1627, form the restaurant, decorated with innumerable antique tiles and brass kettles, carved oak panelling and two Rembrandt etchings. Dinner only.

Dorrius Nieuwe Zijds Voorburgwal 338 (tel: 23-56-75). Opened in 1870, it has been providing hunting stews, cheese croquettes, and everything else Dutch ever since. Closed Sundays.

Die Port Van Cleve Nieuwe Zijds Voorburgwal 178 (tel: 24-00-47) is another traditional Amsterdam restaurant whose specialty is steak.

Indonesian Restaurants

Highly recommended are:

Bali Leidsestraat 95 (tel: 22-78-78). *Rijsttafel* (some of the most expensive but delicious in town) served only in the evening. For lunch try *nasi goreng* (rice with meat) or *bami goreng* (noodles with meat).

Samo Sebo P.C. Hooftstraat 27 (tel: 72-81-46). Closed Sundays.

Sea Place Oosterdokskade 8 (tel: 26-47-77). Floating restaurant serving Indonesian and Chinese food.

Speciaal Nieuwe Leliestraat 142 (tel: 24-97-06) is an intimate cane-decorated restaurant. Dinner only.

SHOPPING

The great thing about Amsterdam is that almost everyone speaks English, especially the young people for whom it is a compulsory school subject. Finding what you want in any of the stores is therefore incredibly easy: if you don't see it, ask. The Dutch are not only courteous but helpful and willing to make the visitor's day a happy one. There is no need to worry about bartering in the markets. The price that is marked is the price!

You won't find supermarkets or hypermarkets in the city centre — most of the food shops are small and villagey. Some of the best fruit and vegetables are on sale in the markets.

Generally, Amsterdam's shops are open from 0900 to 1730 on weekdays with the exception of Mondays, when many do not open until 1300, and Thursdays when most do not close until 2100. There are a number of what are called 'night shops' in the city. They sell foodstuffs, fruit, delicatessen, etc., and have varying opening and closing times. Several are open until midnight or later and many remain open on Sundays.

The best buys must be diamonds and delftware though, in fact, the most popular buys are cheese, chocolates and clogs! North Americans are more likely to find bargains than the British. Americans and Canadians will find in Amsterdam a European shopping centre *par excellence* with all kinds of goods for sale from French fashions to Swiss watches and English antiques. The British are better sticking to locally produced goods. For both markets, it's worth noting that diamond-encrusted watches, for example, may be cheaper to buy here than in Switzerland because the diamonds are added in Holland.

Delftware (with a small d) has become the name for all Dutch hand-painted earthenware pottery which looks like ancient Chinese porcelain, and it can be blue and white, red and white or multi-coloured. Delft Blue, or Delftware (capital D), is mainly blue and white and is made at one factory (with a shop), De Porceleyne Fles, on Muntplein. The genuine article is expensive and mass-produced imitations are found all over the place. Be careful as these are also expensive.

Dutch pewter is decorative and noted for the quality of its design. Filigree silver work abounds in the shops and note that all gold sold in Holland is 14-carat or 18-carat, unlike the UK where 9-carat gold is also available. Dutch crystal from the cities of Leerdam and Maastricht is a good buy, cigars are plentiful and cheap and antiques are found in profusion in the shops of the antique quarter centred on Nieuwe Spiegelstraat.

Shopping in Amsterdam need not be tiring for, although shops are concentrated in certain districts, they are all within walking distance of each other.

Handmade wooden clogs

Cigar shop

Practically everything (that isn't a café) is a store along Kalverstraat, Rokin, Nieuwendijk and Leidsestraat. (Kalverstraat is a pedestrian precinct and Leidsestraat allows only trams.) Nieuwe Spiegelstraat, the centre for antiques, and P.C. Hoofstraat, noted for couture, are both near the Rijksmuseum. An elegant street for fashion and delicatessen shops is Beethovenstraat, near the Amsterdam Hilton in the southern part of the city. The Jordaan area is noted for unusual boutiques and second-hand bargains. Bulbs and beautiful flowers can be bought from the floating flower market on the Singel canal.

If you want to find the nearest beauty salon, look in the local Yellow Pages under *Schoonheids-instituten*, and for supermarkets, check under *Supermarkten*. There is a handy English directory at the back of the Yellow Pages.

Shop Names

Baker's　Bakkerij
Bookshop　Boekwinkel
Butcher's　Slagerij
Cake shop　Banketbakkerij
Chemist/pharmacist　Apotheek/Drogist
Clothing (women's)　Dameskleding
Clothing (men's)　Herenkleding
Clothing (children's)　Kinderkleding
Delicatessen　Same *or* Vleeswaren
Electrical goods　Elektriciteitswinkel
Films (photographic)　Fotografie
Fish shop　Viswinkel
Fruit shop　Fruithandelaar
Grocer's　Kruidenierswinkel
Hairdressers　Schoonheids-instituten
Hardware store　Ijzerhandel/Ijzerwaren
Household goods　Huishoudartikelen
Ice cream parlour　Ijs-salon
Snack bar　Snelbuffet
Shoe shop　Schoenenwinkel
Supermarket　Supermarkt
Sweet shop　Snoep winkel
Tobacconist　Tabakswinkel/Sigarenhandel

Specialty Stores

Scheltema & Holkema, Spuistraat, for specialist books.

Athenaeum Boekhandel, Spuistraat, for books.

Allert de Lange, Damrak, for books including travel guides and maps.

Focke & Meltzer, Kalverstraat, for Delft Blue and Makkum pottery, Royal Holland pewter, fine china, crystal and glass.

Wille, Nieuwendijk, for china and glass.

Zumpolle, Kalverstraat, for leather goods

Bonebakker, Rokin, for fine jewellery.

Schapp, Citroen & Van Gelder, Kalverstraat, for jewellery.

E. Kramer, Nieuwe Spiegelstraat, for antique tiles.

Department Stores

Bijenkorf, Dam Square. Known as the Beehive, this is Amsterdam's Harrods or Bloomingdale's. Expensive, but quality goods of all kinds.

Vroom & Dreesman, Kalverstraat, is the city's number two general department store, offering reasonable prices and quality.

Metz & Co, Keizersgracht, small but elegant store specializing in gifts, Liberty prints, etc.

Peek & Cloppenburg, Dam Square, good selection of quality clothing for men, women and children.

Hema chain stores are found throughout the city, selling everything from make-up to food. Good for inexpensive gifts and children's clothes. (Familiar British store names include C & A, Mothercare, Laura Ashley and Austin Reed.)

Shopping Streets

Kalverstraat, stretching from Dam Square to the Muntplein, is the largest and busiest shopping street in the city. You will find everything but foodstuffs or beauty salons here.

P.C. Hooftstraat is elegant and exclusive, with luxury shops selling haute couture and other fine goods. Stores include national designers Edgar Voss and Fong Leng. This is also the street in which to find Cartier, Godiva, etc. The streets off P.C. Hooftstraat are equally chic.

Antique shop on Prinsengracht

Nieuwe Spiegelstraat (and all the streets beginning with 'Spiegel' in the vicinity) is the main area for antiques, old prints, books, porcelain and furniture.

Markets

Albert Cuypstraat City's biggest general market. (Mon.-Fri. 0900-1800; Sat. 0900-1700).

Amstelveld Plants and flowers on Prinsengracht. (Mon. 1000-1500).

Buikslotermeerplein General market. (Tues.-Fri. 0900-1800; Sat. 0900-1700).

Dapperstraat General. (Mon.-Fri. 0900-1800; Sat. 0900-1700).

De Looier Indoor antique market, Elandsgracht 109. (Mon.-Thurs. 1100-1700; Sat. 0900-1700).

Fazantenhof Bijlmermeer General. (Tues.-Fri. 1000-1800; Sat. 1000-1700).

Gulden Winckelplantsoen General. (Tues.-Fri. 0900-1800; Sat. 0900-1700).

Lindengracht General. (Tues.-Fri. 0900-1300; Sat. 0900-1700).

Nieuwe Zijds Voorburgwal Stamp market. (Wed., Sat. afternoons).

Nieuwmarkt General. (Mon.-Fri. 0900-1800; Sat. 0900-1700).

Noordermarkt Bird market. (Sat. mornings).

Noordermarkt/Westerstraat Textiles and second-hand clothes, accessories, etc. (Mon. 0900-1300).

Oudemanhuispoort Book market. (Mon.-Sat. 1000-1600).

Plein 40-50 General. (Tues.-Fri. 0900-1800; Sat. 0900-1700).

Singel Flower Market (Mon.-Fri. 0900-1900, Thurs. to 2100; Sat. 0900-1700).

Sumatrastraat General. (Sat. 0900-1700).

ten Katestraat General. (Mon.-Fri. 0900-1800; Sat. 0900-1700).

Valkenburgerstraat Famous flea market. Moved here from previous (nearby) location on Waterlooplein. (Mon.-Sat. 1000-1600).

Vespuccistraat General. (Tues.-Fri. 0900-1800; Sat. 0900-1700).

Waterlooplein (see *Valkenburgerstraat*).

ENTERTAINMENT

Amsterdam has always been one of Europe's liveliest night-time cities and the Amsterdammer takes the attitude that anything goes. The tolerance of the city elders was the reason the hippies of the 60s camped here in such numbers and why it is such a popular destination for the gay community today.

But don't get me wrong. The scene is rather more fun than seedy and though there are live sex shows going on in the red-light district, the quarter itself is on *everyone's* sightseeing itinerary.

The main entertainment areas are: Leidseplein, which boasts a lot of discos, cabarets and clubs, Rembrandtsplein and adjacent Thorbeckeplein, and Zeedijk, the old sailors' quarter of the city, and rather bawdy.

Amsterdammers themselves seem to prefer an evening out in a brown café or a bar with music, though the young do flock to the discos in the areas mentioned above. Many of the discos are patronized by the under-21s, except in the top hotels where the age group is generally much older.

Rembrandtsplein

Nightclubs, Cabaret, Discos

Expect to pay an entrance fee, usually higher on weekends. One of the best places for a Las Vegas-style revue, dinner and sequins (for a fixed price), is the *Lido* on Leidseplein. (The Lido has its own canal-side 'beach' with deck chairs and a bar for summer sunning.) *Piccadilly* on Thorbeckeplein is also recommended for its floor show.

Fashionable discos come and go, as they do in any capital city, but *King's Club*, on Korte Leidsedwarsstraat, seems to go on for ever. At the time of writing, one of the 'in' places in the Jordaan is *de Snelbinder* (Dutch for the padlock used on a bicycle). Amsterdam has its first roller disco, near the Bijenkorf department store on Dam Square. The more sophisticated choose a hotel disco such as the *Windjammer* in the Marriott, Stadhouderskade 21, the *Boston Club* in Sonesta, Kattengat 1, or *Juliana's* in the Hilton, Breitnerstraat 3.

Trendy bars also change names and faces, but *Oblomov* on Reguliersdwarsstraat (just behind the Singel flower market) is the current place to go. It has its own garden and attracts a mixed clientele, unlike the other clubs and bars on this street, which are predominantly gay. A lively bar with loud jazz is *Rum Runners* adjacent to Westerkerk.

A new idea in Amsterdam is participation in a 'Brueghel Night' at the restaurant in the Arts and Crafts Centre at Nieuwen-

dijk 16. This is a fixed-price meal with entertainment based on the medieval banquet theme. Although it is primarily suited to large groups (and it is not cheap), individuals are also welcome to make reservations.

Most men 'looking for a good time', to use a hackneyed phrase, would head for the red-light district, but hostess clubs do also exist elsewhere. 'Negotiations' are not compulsory, merely an extra. The most elegant, I'm told, is *Yab Yum* on the Singel.

The Red-Light District

Amsterdam's prostitutes, in unwritten agreement with the law, have settled in one area of the old city, around the Oude Kerk. This district is known as the *Walletjes* (little walls), situated as it is between two high-banked canals, Oudezijds Voorburgwal and Oudezijds Achterburgwal. The ladies-of-the-night, who sit scantily dressed in red-lit windows here, are all registered and they do not walk the streets. When they're 'in business', they simply close their curtains. Such an unusual display proves fascinating for many tourists and it is perfectly safe to walk around here during the day, provided that you skip Zeedijk towards the harbour, as this is a drug users' hangout. Women tourists on foot probably won't feel comfortable in the quarter at night, as it is also the location of the seamier clubs.

Cultural Nightlife

Best places to get tickets are the AUB office in Stadsschouwburg (Municipal Theatre), Leidseplein 1, open Monday-Saturday 1000-1800; and the VVV office Stationsplein 10, open Monday-Saturday 1000-1600. The VVV office has a special Theatre Ticket Department which can

Carré Theatre on the Amstel

Stadsschouwburg (Muncicipal Theatre)

arrange reservations nationwide and it also issues, in English, *This Week in Amsterdam*, a weekly publication listing all events and entertainments in the city. You can telephone enquiries, but not bookings, by ringing (AUB) 22-90-11 or (VVV) 26-64-44.

General starting times are: opera 2000, ballet, theatre, etc., 2015, pop concerts 2100-2230. On Sundays most theatres have a matinee 1400-1500.

The Holland Culture Card (so far available only to US and Canadian visitors) gives free or reduced admission to many museums and galleries and allows last-minute purchase of tickets to concerts, opera and ballet. It also gives discount travel on Dutch trains. This card cannot be obtained in Holland but must be bought before leaving home. For further information contact the Netherlands National Tourist Office.

Music Some 12,500 performances of the arts take place annually in Amsterdam which is as liberal in its culture as it is in all other areas. The main pride and attraction is the Concertgebouw (concert hall), a landmark on Museumplein. It has excellent acoustics and has known such famous conductors as Gustav Mahler and Richard Strauss. The Concertgebouw Orchestra, under its principal conductor, Bernard Haitink, performs from mid-September through March, but recitals, chamber music and pop concerts are held here throughout the year. In summer there are behind-the-scene tours of this celebrated building (1888) and, during the annual Holland Festival (throughout June), many memorable events take place here.

You may be lucky enough to find free lunchtime concerts at the Concertgebouw – check the English publication, *This Week in Amsterdam*, to find out. On Sun-

day mornings, for a very low admission price, coffee concerts are given in the restored 17th-century Lutheran Church, on Kattengat, which nowadays is the Sonesta Hotel's conference hall. (The concerts are open to the general public.) Other free lunchtime concerts are held at the IJsbreker, Weesperzijde 13, centre for contemporary music.

Theatre The city's oldest and most illustrious theatre is the Stadsschouwburg (Municipal Theatre) on Leidseplein, *the* place for ballet, dance, opera and operetta. Its history goes back to 1638 and innumerable celebrities have played on the stage here. The three resident companies are: The Netherlands Opera, the Dutch National Ballet and the repertory group, *Publiekstheater*.

Most legitimate theatre is performed in Dutch, though English-language productions are sometimes given at the Mickery on Rozengracht, and musicals are featured at the Carré Theatre on the Amstel. It is also worth checking what is playing at Centrum-Bellevue on Leidsekade, Shaffy Theater on Keizersgracht and Theater de Suikerhof on Prinsengracht. Besides these better-known theatres, the city also has a host of small café theatres which you'll find listed in *This Week in Amsterdam*.

Lovers of the arts should note that the **Holland Festival** (which has been going since 1947) is held during the first three weeks of June every year. There is something to appeal to everyone as events include ballet, concerts, plays, recitals, films and street happenings.

Film Cinemas are plentiful in Amsterdam – the largest is on Leidseplein. There is little language problem for the visitor as all films in the city are shown in their original language and, since a host of them are American-made, you're in luck.

SPORTS

Athletics events take place at the following stadiums: Ajax Stadium, Middenweg 401, 1098, tel: 94-65-15; Olympic Stadium, Stadionplein, 1076, tel: 71-11-15; Sporthal Zuid, IJsbaanpad 19, 1076, tel: 73-13-14.

Bowling can be played at the Bowling Centre Knijn B.V., Scheldeplein 3, 1078, tel: 64-22-11.

Cycling Bikes are easy to rent (addresses on p. 15), can be carried on trains, or used for organized itineraries. Between April and November there is a host of cycling events, including the Landelijke Fietsdag (National Cycling Event) on the first or second Saturday in May.

Golf Guests may play by arrangement at the Amsterdamse Golfclub, Zwartelaantje 4, 1099 CE, tel: 94-36-50. Situated close to the Bijlmermeer, south east of the city, this 18-hole course is open all year. Green fees are higher on weekends than during the week, though purchase of a weekly ticket is possible. A practice ground is available here.

Not far from Amsterdam, the Kennemer Golf and Country Club in Zandvoort, Kennemerweg 78-80, 2042 XT, tel: 02597-12836, is a typical seaside 18-hole course.

Horse Riding is possible in Amsterdamse Bos, south of the city. Riding indoors, by the hour, can be arranged with B.V. Amsterdamse Manege, Amsterdamse Bos, Nieuwe Kalfjeslaan 25, Amstelveen, tel: 43-13-42.

Mini Golf can be played in summer at Amstelpark, Amsterdamse Bos and Sloterpark.

Rowing There is a rowing course in Amsterdamse Bos, south of the city.

Sailing Boats may be rented from Twellegae, Nieuwendammerdijk 282, tel: 32-48-77.

Skating Jaap Edenbaan, Radioweg 64, 1098, is open from October to March.

Squash can be played at the Sportcentre Borchland, Holterbergweg Duivendrecht 8-12, tel: 96-14-41, and at Frans Otten-stadion, Stadionstraat 10, 1076, tel: 72-87-67.

Swimming Outdoor (open May-August) and indoor pools are located at Floraparkbad, Sneeuwbalweg 5, 1032, tel: 36-81-23; Mirandabad, de Mirandalaan 9, 1079, tel: 42-80-80;   and   Sloterparkbad, Slotermeerlaan, 1064, tel: 13-37-00. Outdoor public pools are also located at Brediusbad, Spaarndammerdijk 306, 1013, tel: 82-91-16; Flevoparkbad, Zeeburgerdijk 630, 1095, tel: 92-50-30; and Jan van Galenbad, Jan van Galenstraat 315, 1056, tel:

12-80-01. Indoor public pools are located at Sportfondsenbadoost, Fronemanstraat 3, 1093, tel: 65-08-11; Sportfondsenbad West, Cornelis Dirkszstraat 11, 1056, tel: 18-89-11; and Zuiderbad, Hobbemastraat 26, 1071, tel: 79-22-17. Many hotels in the city have their own pools and health clubs.

Tennis Public courts are found in the city's parks and several hotels have their own courts.

Sports events are published only in the Dutch newspapers such as *Het Parool* or *Het Nieuwe.* Chess, darts and billiards are played in many of the cafés.

YOUNG AMSTERDAM

Where to Stay

Amsterdam has always been a mecca for young travellers and it is well used to the budget that can't be overdrawn. The 'hotelette', a simple small hotel, is not classified, sometimes because it doesn't offer bedrooms with bathroom attached or perhaps because it doesn't have a lift but it is one of the least expensive types of accommodation. There are in addition youth hostels and student hotels, education centres and sleep-ins, campsites and exchange programmes.

The VVV offices have complete lists of budget accommodation but here is a selection: Jeugdhotel Adam en Eva, Sarphatistraat 105, 1018 GA, tel: 24-62-06. Studentenhotel Adolesce, Nieuwe Keizersgracht 26, 1018 DS, tel: 26-39-59. ACRO Low Budget, Jan Luijkenstraat 42-44 1071 CR, tel: 62-05-26. Bob's Youth Hotel, NZ Voorburgwal 92, 1012 SG, tel 23-00-63. Cok Young Budget, Koningslaan 1, 1075 AA, tel: 64-61-11. Jeugdhotel Eben Haezer, Bloemstraat 179 1016, tel: 24-47-17. Hans Brinker Hotel Kerkstraat 136, 1017 GR, tel: 22-06-88 Jeugdhotel Kabul, Warmoesstraat 42 1012 JE, tel: 23-71-58. Jeugdhotel The Shelter, Barndesteeg 21-25, 1012 BV, tel 25-32-30. In 1985 the price range was about Dfl 14-25 a night.

Sleep-ins are geared to students although no membership is necessary and there is no age limit. Guests need their own sleeping bags and accommodation in dormitory style, but there is a storage room for luggage, space for bikes, lots of showers and usually a lounge where films are sometimes shown, plus a small snack bar. Advance reservations cannot be made for sleep-ins and they are open only in the summer. There is one on Mauritskade 28 tel: 94-74-44.

Youth hostels include the Stadsdoelen

Kloveniersburgwal 97, 1011 KB, tel: 24-68-32, which is open March-October; the Vondelpark, Zandpad 5, 1054 GA, tel: 83-17-44, which is open all year. No-one is allowed to sleep out in the open air but two campsites catering for youth are: Vliegenbos, Meeuwenlaan 138, 1022 AM, tel: 36-88-55; and Zeeburg, IJdijk, tel: 94-66-88. Both of these are open April-September.

An organization which finds guest house accommodation (lodgings as a paying guest with a family) is ISOK, Jan Tooropstraat 4, 2225 XT, Katwijk aan Zee, tel: 01718-13533. The Cultural Exchange Programme for Youth helps with arrangements for 16-18 year olds, organizes work programmes for the under 28s and also organizes language and other educational courses. The Amsterdam address is: Keizersgracht 722, 1017 EW, tel: 22-09-16.

Other helpful organizations include: BIJK, P.O. Box 15344, 1001 MH Amsterdam, tel: 25-08-21, which will give you information about exchanges, courses and work opportunities. The International Youth Exchange Foundation offers work programmes to 18-25 year olds wishing to spend a year in Holland. Write to the Secretariat Information Workgroup: P.O. Box 501, 6800 AM Arnhem, tel: 085-454649. (When writing, enclose an international reply coupon.)

Food and Drink

Amsterdam is one European capital where you won't faint from lack of nourishment or the final tab. Anyone staying on a bed and breakfast basis can be sure that the breakfast, though cold, will be hearty. The sandwich shops *(broodjeswinkels)* sell a great variety of sandwiches at reasonable prices, and look out for *mensas*, or day menus, which are aimed at students. There is one to be found on Damstraat and one not far from the flea market, but many brown cafés also offer day menus — perhaps hamburgers with two vegetables. Examples include De Pilserij, De Reiger and Eet Tuin cafés.

Several city restaurants feature a fixed-price tourist menu (see list on p. 18). The VVV also recommends the following for young people: *Cantharel*, Kerkstraat 377; *Carre Kelder*, Amstel 133; *H88*, Herengracht 88; *Ashoka*, Geldersekade 23; *Keuken van 1870*, Spuistraat 4; *Kosmos Macrobiotic Food*, Prins Hendrikkade 142; *De Lantaarn*, 2e Constantijn Huygensstraat 64, and the *Mensa Academica*, Damstraat 3.

Beer or local gin are the cheapest alcoholic beverages but the Dutch drink a great deal of coffee which you'll find available just about everywhere.

Of course, knowing what to order, is the

Café on Leidseplein

best key to eating on a budget. In addition to the sandwiches *(broodjes)* already mentioned, look out for an *uitsmijter* for lunch or as an evening snack in a pub. Literally translated, the word means 'throw outer' or 'bouncer' and originally it was pub food offered to help patrons sober up. It comprises slices of buttered bread topped with ham, cheese or roast beef and one or two fried eggs. The Dutch often order a *Koffietafel* lunch which is simply another breakfast plus a bowl of soup or salad. Other excellent, inexpensive snacks to look out for are the *saucijzenbrood* (sausage roll) and *croquetten* (meat or cheese croquettes). Pancake houses are another good bet. They serve all kinds of crêpe, savoury or sweet.

Bargains are plentiful in all the city's Asian restaurants, particularly Indonesian or Chinese. At others, ask if they have a *kleine kaart* menu offering snacks or the dish of the day. This, too, will help keep prices within reason.

If you're looking for atmosphere, try the canalside bistro restaurants. There are now many of them, often renovated canal mansions and warehouses dating back to the 17th and 18th centuries. One such is the beamed and tiled *Bols Tavern*, Rozengracht 106, a stone's throw from Anne Frank House and Westerkerk. Also recommended in the vicinity are: *Pilpenia*, 23 Westermarkt, a cosy, candlelit place with Dutch murals on the wall. *De Belhamel*, Brouwersgracht 60, has one of the prettiest locations in Amsterdam, on the Brewers' canal. Thirty types of pancake are listed in *The Pancake Bakery* at Prinsengracht 191, a restored canalside cellar, and *De Zoete Inval*, at Herengracht 309, is a simple spot for inexpensive omelettes.

There is no focal point for budget eating places — they're scattered about almost everywhere. Young people like the cafés near the Singel flower market or the lively atmosphere on Leidseplein — the terrace outside Broodje van Kootje, Leidseplein 20, for instance, is one of the best meeting places. Look for the daily specials at *Café du Centre*, Leidsestraat 80, the budget version of the well-known Dikker & Thijs restaurant. Pastries are delicious at *W. Berkhoff*, Leidsestraat 46, and big, bustling *Heineken Hoek* on Leidseplein has a wide-ranging menu which includes three daily specials.

If you're museum visiting, you'll be around Museumplein. In this vicinity you can eat on a shoestring at *Hopsy*, P.C. Hooftstraat 63, or *Heyenbrock's Sandwich Shop* at P.C. Hooftstraat 86. The museums' own cafeterias are an alternative. Both the Van Gogh and the Stedelijk have garden terraces open in summer. If you are shopping on Kalverstraat, try *Breem's Coffee Corner*, Spui 10A, next to the Begijnhof department store. They offer 14 kinds of coffee plus various crêpes and salads. Inexpensive toasted sandwiches can be bought in the blue-tiled *Scaramouche Petit Restaurant*, next to the Royal Palace, and many young people flock to *Frascati* at Nes 59, just behind Rokin, for a hearty soup or *uitsmijter*. University students like the modest prices and filling food at *Bistro Markus*, Oude Zijds Voorburgwal 250, and there is a long menu at *Duke's Restaurant*, Damrak 5, near Centraal Station.

Shopping

The best section of town for boutique browsing is the Jordaan. It used to be the working-class quarter and is still full of brown cafés, but today it is a desirable area in which to live and *the* place where budding fashion designers wish to set up in business.

If you're looking for basics, head for any of the Hema chain stores. The prices are reasonable and the quality is good — along the lines of Marks and Spencer. For books and records, try the Nieuwendijk, Kalverstraat and the surrounding streets.

For bargains try the markets. The biggest general market is at Albert Cuypstraat, open every day, except Sunday, year round from 0900-1800 (Mon.-Fri.) 0900-1700 (Sat.). Expect to find inexpensive clothing and accessories here as well as fresh food. (See also Shopping.)

Entertainment

Many of Amsterdam's old pubs are neighbourhood places, often providing free entertainment from singer, pianist or accordion player. In any case, they're fun to meet and mingle in. One of the most popular with students is *Hoppe*, Spui 20, always spilling over with a lively crowd.

Jazz clubs, usually pretty spartan in decor but with a zesty atmosphere, are another favourite. You're rarely pushed to keep buying drinks so one coke could pay for an evening's entertainment. Recommended are *Runn-Inn*, a jazz café at Keizersgracht 402, and *Joseph Lam's Jazzclub*, Laagte Kadijk 35, a converted warehouse, close to the harbour, featuring Dixieland.

Discos rarely charge an entrance fee, except perhaps on the weekend, and there is no cover charge. In discos outside of hotels, drink prices are not exorbitant and the crowd is young. A popular disco is *Zorba de Buddha Rajneesh*, Oude Zijds Voorburgwal 216, a short walk from Dam Square. *De Snelbinder* is a modern disco in Jordaan and there is a roller disco (called *Wijlpaard*) near the Bijenkorf department store. For pop groups and modern theatre, *Paradiso*, Weteringschans 6-8, and *De Melkweg*, Lijnbaansgracht 234a, are both good.

Films are screened in their original language so you'll find plenty in English. The largest cinema complex is on Leidseplein. Only a few plays are performed in English but there are plenty of concert and ballet performances, especially during the annual Holland Festival in June.

The VVV offices have lists of events and publish *This Week in Amsterdam*, a useful list of entertainments and other information.

The AUB in the Municipal Theatre on Leidseplein publish a monthly entertainments guide, *Uitkrant*. It is in Dutch but easy for the visitor to follow. Students with passes can get discounts on theatre and opera tickets.

There are summer festivities every July in the Koepel quarter of town and, in winter, the main outdoor terrace on Leidseplein becomes an ice rink. (See also Entertainment.)

Public transport is cheap in the city and everything operates until midnight after which special night buses take over. One-day and other passes are available. (See Getting Around.)

CHILDREN'S AMSTERDAM

What with 'gingerbread' houses and wooden clogs, Amsterdam sometimes seems made for children. It's child-sized. While there is no English publication or phone number to call to tell you about specific events for children and most of the performances aimed at youngsters are in Dutch, there is still plenty to see and do.

Children aged 4-9 pay half fare on public transport; those aged 10-18 pay about three-quarters of the adult fare.

Things to See

Artis Zoo Plantage Kerklaan. One of the city's top attractions, the zoo contains a host of animals from all over the world and most of them can be seen uncaged in the open. Of special interest is De Wereld der Duisternis (The World of Darkness), where nocturnal animals are on view. There is also a children's farm for petting the more familiar, friendly animals. Attached to the zoo is an aquarium housing a wide variety of sea and river life, including more than 700 species of fish.

The zoo dates from 1838 and covers an area of 10 hectares/25 acres housing some 6000 animals, among which are species rarely found in zoos or in danger of extinction, e.g., the orang-utan and ruffed and ring-tailed lemurs. The 19th-century garden atmosphere (despite constant expansion) is reflected in the zoo's full name, Natura Artis Magistra: nature is the teacher of the arts. Open daily 0900-1700 with special prices for children.

Aviodome Schiphol Airport. A museum devoted to the history of man's efforts to fly. The Aviodome, very close to the arrival terminal, features models, mock-ups of projected supersonic planes and space shuttles, plus many original old aircraft. Children can also test their pilot skills here on a link trainer which simulates flying. Open daily 1000-1700 (Apr.-Oct.), Tuesday-Sunday 1000-1700 (Nov.-Mar.). Reduced entrance price for children.

Dolls' Houses at Rijksmuseum Museumplein. The ground floor of this major museum contains a collection of beautifully furnished, 17th-century dolls' houses. Open Tuesday-Saturday 1000-1700, Sundays and holidays 1300-1700.

Kindermuseum TM Junior (Children's Museum) Linnaeusstraat 2. Opened in 1975, this museum was designed for children. It features exhibitions and programmes about the Third World and our connections with it. Most of the exhibits can be touched and youngsters may work, dance, play music and make pottery inside the museum. Ideal on Sunday afternoons and holiday times (when school groups are not visiting) for 6-12 year olds. Programmes run from 1300-1530.

Madame Tussaud Kalverstraat 156. Find out if you're taller than Rembrandt by standing next to his wax model. Like Tussaud's elsewhere, this museum contains a prestigious set of people in wax. The models in the Hall of Mirrors are of

Sightseeing boats on Keizersgracht

people who have made their mark on the world, such as John F. Kennedy and Indira Gandhi. There is an entertainment department, a historical department and a whole room devoted to Rembrandt. And you can see how wax models are made in the workshop. Open daily 1000-1800.

Scheepvaartmuseum Kattenburgerplein 1. A maritime museum which should appeal to all age groups. Old ships and many models are displayed here. There is a collection of old weapons and indeed everything that was vital to sailing in the past, including many maps and globes. Open Tuesday-Saturday 1000-1700, Sundays 1300-1700.

Spaarpottenmuseum Raadhuisstraat 20. The Money Box Museum is located just behind the Royal Palace and contains around 12,000 money boxes from all over the world: piggy banks, 500-year-old coin collections from Indonesia, imaginative pottery money boxes and intricate gold and silver ones. Open Monday-Friday 1300-1600.

Zeiss Planetarium Kromwijkdreef 11, 1108 JA. Open Wednesdays 1200-1730, weekends 0930-1730. Programmes about the stars are given hourly. Near the planetarium is a popular park, Gaasperplas, which has a water playground.

Out of Doors

Canal boat trips are just as likely to appeal to children as adults. The canal 'buses' glide along smoothly and don't make you sea sick. Nor does it matter if there is a shower as you're under cover of a glass roof. There are many wharves and a good variety of sightseeing excursions to choose from. Trips last from one hour to an afternoon's excursion.

The barrel organ can still be seen and heard in the streets today

From June to mid-September, the towers of the Oude Kerk (1000-1700 hrs) and the Westerkerk (1400-1700 hrs) are open to the public. It's a long climb to the top but the view is worth it.

As for parks, Amsterdam can boast about 20 within the city limits. Some, such as Sarphati Park, are little more than a green patch with trees and flowers but others, such as Vondel, are full of amusements for young and old alike. Picnicking and sports facilities and open-air theatre are all featured in Vondel. King of them all, as far as children are concerned, is the Amsterdamse Bos (Amsterdam Wood) which runs south from the capital to the residential town of Amstelveen. This is an enormous recreational area with trails for horse riding and paths for cycling, a rowing course, tennis courts, sports fields, picnic and camping grounds and special hiking trails. It was created during the Depression in 1929 when thousands of the unemployed were put to work on the project. Ever since, the area has been continually enlarged and developed. A map of the whole area is available from the Bos Museum or the campsite. The Beatrix Park is another in the city's southern quarter, with canals and climbing frames.

Entertainment

Several cinemas run morning and after-noon children's film programmes each week, usually on a Wednesday, Saturday and Sunday. These include Cineac, Reguliersbreestraat 31, and Rialto, Centuurbaan 338.

Dutch snacks will probably appeal to even the smallest toddler when they're as sweet as a *poffertje*, a very small, iced pancake. And Dutch ice cream is delicious too.

Shops

De Bijenkorf (the Beehive) department store on Dam Sq. has one of the best toy departments in town. A wide range of quality items for all ages can be found at Kerkelbach & Co., Kalverstraat 30, and the ground floor of Metz & Co., Keizersgracht 455, is good for toys and unusual gifts. For the novelty toy or gift, try Sam-Sam, Singel 406, it's a children's toy boutique. The under-fives are well taken care of by Speel-Goed, Nes 102, and the family-run 't Speelgoedhuis, Beethovenstraat 58, stocks a good selection of educational toys.

Other shops recommended by the VVV are as follows:

It's Raining Cats and Dogs Reestraat 24, tel: 23-80-18, which sells all kinds of items from mugs to pens, all featuring dog and cat designs.

Kinderboekhandel 1e Bloemstraat 23, tel: 22-47-61, for children's books.

Lambiek Kerkstraat 78, tel: 26-75-43, offering comics in all languages.

Turquoise Tomahawk, Berenstraat 16, tel: 25-71-06, all kinds of Indian things.

't Japanese Winkeltje Nieuwe Zijds Voorburgwal 175, tel: 27-95-23, for all things Japanese.

Het Treinenhuis Bilderdijkstraat 94, tel: 18-12-55, all items to do with trains.

Jack in the Box J.P. Heyestraat 85, tel: 85-12-88, great buys in second-hand toys.

Panda Boutique, Brouwersgracht 54, tel: 92-20-84. This is the shop of the World Wildlife Fund.

WHAT YOU NEED TO KNOW

Chemists/Pharmacies are generally open 0800/0900 to 1730/1800, Monday-Friday, with rotation duty during evenings, nights and weekends. For information about weekend duty call 13-28-55. None of the pharmacies is open 24 hours, but you can call the doctors' service (64-21-11) to find out your nearest open shop.

Churches Churches of all denominations are to be found in Amsterdam. They are listed in the local newspapers and some are listed in Useful Addresses (p. 31).

Closing Days and Times Most shops are open 0830/0900 to 1730/1800 Monday-Friday, and on Saturday to 1700. Not all shops open on a Saturday but the markets are almost all open at the weekend. Closing days vary but usual store closings are Monday mornings or Wednesday afternoons. Some stores close at lunchtime. There are special 'night shops' for food buying, and a list is available from the VVV. Late night shopping is Thursday or Friday till 2100. Major museums close on Mondays.

Diamonds The following give free tours of diamond works: Amsterdam Diamond Center, Rokin 1, 1012 KK, tel: 24-57-87. Open daily 1000-1730, on Thursday to 2030. Coster Diamonds, Paulus Potterstraat 2-4, 1071 CZ, tel: 76-22-22. Open daily 1030 and 1430. Gassan Diamond House, Nieuwe Achtergracht 17-23, 1018 XV, tel: 22-53-33. Open daily 0900-1730. Holshuysen-Stoeltie B.V., Wagenstraat 13-17, 1017 CZ, tel: 23-76-01. Open daily 0900-1700. Van Moppes Diamant, Albert Cuypstraat 2-6, 1072 CT, tel: 76-12-42. Open daily 0830-1700; Sundays in summer 0900-1700.

Electricity 220-volt, 50-cycle current is standard and you may need an adaptor. Better hotels are equipped with, or will lend, a hairdryer and will press clothes for a minimal charge.

Get in Touch with the Dutch This is the name of a special programme for foreign visitors who wish to make personal contact with Dutch families and/or business people. The VVV will make the arrangements.

Handicapped Facilities for the handicapped are excellent in the Netherlands and include special toilets in motorway restaurants and museums and ramps at the entrances to public buildings of interest. Dutch paper money has dots on it so that the blind can distinguish between the various denominations.

Health The Central Medical Service will provide information on doctors, dentists, pharmacists, tel: 64-21-11. The Municipal Health Service may be reached on 5-55-55-55. First aid is available at the Academisch Medisch, Meibergdreef 9, 1105, tel; 5-66-91-11; V.U. Ziekenhuis, de Boelelaan 1117, 1081, tel: 5-48-91-11; Lucas Ziekenhuis, Jan Tooropstraat 164, 1061, tel: 5-10-89-11; Onze Lieve Vrouwe Gasthuis, 1e Oosterparkstraat 179, 1091, tel:5-99-91-11; Slotervaart Ziekenhuis, Louwesweg 6, 1066, tel: 5-12-93-33. (See also Insurance p. 10.)

Lost Property If property is lost on a train, go to the *Verloren Voorwerpen* office at any station. After ten days the goods from all over Holland go to Concordiastraat 70, Utrecht. For property lost on the buses, trams or metro, see the GVB Head Office, Prins Hendrikkade 108-114, P.O. Box 2131, 1000 CC Amsterdam. For anything lost in the street or parks, see the police: Gebouw Saskia, Waterlooplein 11, tel: 5-59-25-50.

Newspapers and Magazines A number of central bookstands in the city and in top hotels sell English publications. *This Week in Amsterdam* is a useful entertainments guide issued by the VVV.

Police The Dutch police wear dark blue uniforms with a dark blue cap. Headquarters is at Elandsgracht 117, 1016 TT, tel: 5-59-91-11. There are other police stations at Lijnbaansgracht, tel: 5-59-23-03, and at Warmoesstraat 44-46, tel: 5-59-22-03. In case of emergency dial 22-22-22.

Postal Services Stamps may be purchased at post offices, some hotels and from tobacconists. The main general post office is located at Nieuwe Zijds Voorburgwal 182, 1012 SJ, tel: 5-55-89-11. It is open daily 0830-1800, on Thursday to 2030, and on Saturday 0900-1200. For long-distance calls and telegrams it is open 24 hours daily. This post office does not accept packages, the Post Office, Oosterdokskade (open Monday-Friday 0830-2100, Saturday 0900-1200) deals with parcel post.

Postal rates are on view at all post

offices. Amsterdam's letter boxes are mostly red. Two boxes hang side by side on the walls. Look for the one saying *Streek*, for mail within the city or its surroundings, and the other saying *Overige*, for all other destinations.

Public Holidays New Year's Day, Good Friday, Easter Sunday and Monday, Queen's Birthday (30 April), Ascension Day, Whit Sunday and Monday, Christmas Day and Boxing Day. Also, every five years, Liberation Day on 5 May (next in 1990).

Telephones and Telegrams International direct-dial calls may be made from the general post office, all top hotels, or from one of the city's green-coloured telephone kiosks. Many kiosks accept guilders as well as cent coins. Once you have inserted the minimum money and heard the dialling tone, dial the international code number 09. Again wait for dialling tone, then dial the country code, area code and local phone number, inserting more coins as necessary. If you want information about making a call dial 0018. Operator assisted international calls cannot be made from a telephone booth; for local operator calls dial 0010.

Time The Netherlands is on Central European Time, i.e. Greenwich Mean Time (GMT) plus one hour in winter, two in summer. American and Canadian visitors will be putting their watches ahead. Amsterdam is 6 hours ahead of east coast USA, 9 hours ahead of west coast.

Tipping Tipping is pretty much up to yourself in Holland since all hotels, restaurants, taxis, hair salons, etc., must include 15 per cent service by law. What most visitors (and, indeed, the Dutch) do, however, is round off bills to the nearest guilder, i.e., leave small change. It is also general practice to tip hotel porters (even though the bill does include a service charge), doormen who get you a cab, and toilet attendants.

Toilets Public toilets are of a high standard in Holland and can be found in and around major museums and sights, in restaurants and bars, and at motorway filling stations. They are free, though you may wish to leave coinage if someone is in attendance. They are marked *Dames* (women) or *Heren* (men) and/or the internationally recognized symbols for 'ladies' and 'gents'.

Weather Holland has a maritime climate with pleasant summers and mild winters, generally speaking. In August average temperature is around 20°C/69°F, in December about 6°C/42°F. The least rain falls in February, March, April and May. For weather information in Holland call 003. For the time call 002 and for road conditions (070) 31-31-31. (Please note that all information is given in the Dutch language.)

WORDS & PHRASES

Do you speak English?   Spreekt u engels?
Good morning   Goede morgen
Please   Alstublieft
Thank you   Dank u
Yes   Ja
No   Nee
I'm sorry   Het spijt me
Gentlemen   Heren
Ladies   Dames
No smoking   Verboden te roken
It's free   Het is gratis

I'm ill   Ik ben zick
It hurts   Het doet pijn
Every day   Elke dag
Hospital   Ziekenhuis
Dentist   Tandarts
Date of birth   Geboortedatum
Signature   Handtekening

A room   Een kamer
The fixed-price menu   Het vastgestelde menu
How much?   Hoeveel?
Breakfast   Ontbijt
Bacon and eggs   Eieren met spek
Soap   Zeep
Towel   Handdoek
Waiter!   Ober!
Rare   Niet gaar
Medium   Half gaar
Well done   Goed gaar
Roasted   Gebraden
Smoked   Gerookt
Stewed   Gestoofd
Bread   Brood
Toast   Geroosterd brood
Sausages   Worstjes
Chicken   Kip
Lamb   Lamsvlees
Pork   Varkensvlees
Fish   Vis
Rice   Rijst
Peas   Erwtjes
Carrots   Worteltjes
Cauliflower   Bloemkool
Salt   Zout
Dessert   Nagerecht
Ice cream   Ijs
Cheese   Kaas
Wine   Wijn
A bottle   Een fles
Some more wine   Nog wat wijn
Ashtray   Asbak
The bill   De rekening
Is service included?   Es het inclusief?

How do I get to?   Hoe kom ik naar?
Bus stop   Bushalte

Timetable   Dienstregeling
One-way ticket   Enkele reis
Return ticket   Retour
First class   Eerste klas
Second class   Tweede klas
My tickets   Mijn kaartjes
Entrance   Ingang
Exit   Uitgang
Platform   Perron
Stopping at all stations   Stoptreinen
A plan of the town   Een stadsplan
My car   Mijn auto
Carpark   Parkeerterrein
Wait   Wacht
First left/right   Eerste links/rechts
Straight on   Reechtdoor
There   Daar
At the traffic lights Bij de verkeerslichten
Slow   Langzaam
Maximum speed   Maximum snelheid
One-way street   Eenrichtingsverkeer
Crossroads   Kruispunt
Level crossing   Spoorwegkruising
Grade crossing (US)   Spoorwegkruising

Travel agent   Reisburo
Youth hostel   Jeugdherberg
Swimming pool   Zwembad
Hairdresser   Kapper
Dry cleaner   Stomerij
Laundry   Wasserij
Sweet shop   Snoep winkel
Post office   Postkantoor
Stamp   Postzegal
Airmail   Luchtpost

If you want to know more, Collins pocket-size *Dutch Phrase Book* gives comprehensive coverage with a guide to pronunciation for the visitor.

USEFUL ADDRESSES

Tourist Offices
Netherlands National Tourist Office 143 New Bond St., London, tel: 499-9367; 575 Fifth Ave., N.Y. 10036, tei: 245-5320; 681 Market St., San Francisco, tel: 781-3387; 1 Dundas Street West, Suite 2108, Toronto M5G, Ontario 123, tel: 598-2830.
VVV Tourist Offices Stationsplein 10, tel: 26-64-44; Leidseplein 15; Rijksweg A2.

Embassies and Consulates
UK Consulate Koningslaan 44, P.O. Box 5488, 1007 AL Amsterdam, tel: (020) 76-43-43.
US Consulate Museumplein 19, 1071 DJ Amsterdam, tel: (020) 79-03-21.
Canadian Embassy Sophialaan 7, 2514 JP Den Haag, tel: (070) 61-41-11.
Australian Embassy Koninginnegracht 23, 2514 AB Den Haag, tel: (070) 63-09-83.
New Zealand Embassy Mauritskade 25, 2514 HD Den Haag, tel: (070) 46-93-24.
South African Embassy Wassenaarseweg 36, 2596 Den Haag, tel: (070) 65-99-05.
Eire Embassy Willemskade 23, 3016 DM Rotterdam, tel: (010) 14-33-22.

Travel Information
National Reservation Centre (for accommodation), P.O. Box 404, 2260 KA Leidschendam, tel: (070) 20-25-00.
GVB Head Office Scheepvaarthuis, Prins Hendrikkade 108-114, 1011 AK Amsterdam, tel: 5-51-49-11. For information about city transport tel: 27-27-27 (0700-2300 hrs).
Central Taxi Office tel: 77-77-77.
Netherlands Railway Centraal Station, Stationsplein 1, 1012 AB Amsterdam, tel: 23-83-83.
KLM Leidseplein 1, Amsterdam, tel: 43-42-42.
GWK (money exchange) Centraal Station, daily 0800-2245.
Central Medical Service tel: 64-21-11.

Church Services
Begijnhofkerk (Roman Catholic), Begijnhof 29, tel: 22-19-18. Sunday 1100 (French), 1200 (English).
English Reformed Church Begijnhof, tel: 24-96-65. Sunday 1030/1900 (English).
Church of England (Christ Church), Groenburgwal 42, tel: 24-88-77. Sunday 1030 (English).
Duits Evengelische Gemeente (German Evangelic Parish), J.J. Viottastraat 44, tel: 73-25-22. Sunday 1030 (German).
Waalse Kerk (French Reformed Church), Walenpleintje 159, tel: 23-20-74. Sunday 1100 (French).
St Nicolaaskerk (Roman Catholic), Prins Hendrikkade 73, tel: 24-87-49/25-88-53. Sunday 1100.
De Papegaai (Roman Catholic). Kalverstraat 58, tel: 23-18-89. Sunday 0900/1045/1215.
Westerkerk (Reformed), Prinsengracht 281, tel: 24-77-66. Sunday 1030.
Oude Kerk (Reformed), Oudekerksplein, tel: 24-91-83. Sunday 1100.

EVENTS

Feb. Artis Zoo flower exhibition.
Feb./March The Antiques Fair held in the Nieuwe Kerk, Dam Square.
Feb./March The Amsterdam Carnival Parade.
March Amsterdam Art Weeks. A programme of cultural events held in the city's theatres and concert halls.
30 April The Queen's Birthday. All-day celebrations, including a free market throughout the city, a fairground on the

Dam, and fireworks at 2300 hours.

May Amsterdam International Marathon.

May-Oct. Organ recitals in many of the old churches, including Oude Kerk and Nieuwe Kerk.

June Holland Festival (first three weeks). A cultural programme encompassing the new and the traditional in music, dance and drama.

June Amsterdam Canal Race.

June-Aug. Vondelpark Open Air Theatre. Free performances of children's theatre, dance and music.

July Koepelkwartier Street Party.

July Summer Festival. A festival of modern theatre in all the small theatres of Amsterdam.

Aug. Amsterdam7.., a football event involving top European clubs. (Every year the number gets higher. At the time of writing it was 711.)

Sept. Aalsmeer-Amsterdam Bloemencorso. The world's largest and most spectacular flower pageant.

Sept. Jordaan Festival. Convivial street party.

Oct./Nov. Jumping Amsterdam: an indoor horse event.

Nov. The St. Nicholas Parade, when St. Nicholas (patron saint of the city and the Dutch Father Christmas) docks at Amsterdam from Spain with presents for the children.

In 1986 Amsterdam commemorates 400 years of the diamond industry. Also the new Town Hall/Opera House is due to open and major performers from around the world will be here.

Buskers in Dam Square

Het Lieverdje *'Little Darling'*

Amsterdam City Maps

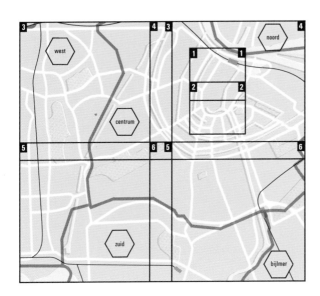

Key to Symbols

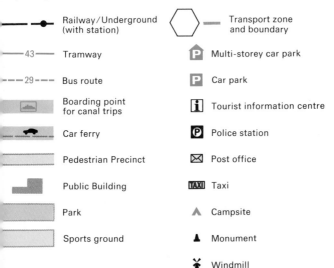

Railway/Underground (with station)	Transport zone and boundary
Tramway 43	Multi-storey car park
Bus route 29	Car park
Boarding point for canal trips	Tourist information centre
Car ferry	Police station
Pedestrian Precinct	Post office
Public Building	Taxi
Park	Campsite
Sports ground	Monument
	Windmill

These maps are adapted with kind permission from the Hallwag city map series

© Wm. Collins Sons & Co. Ltd.

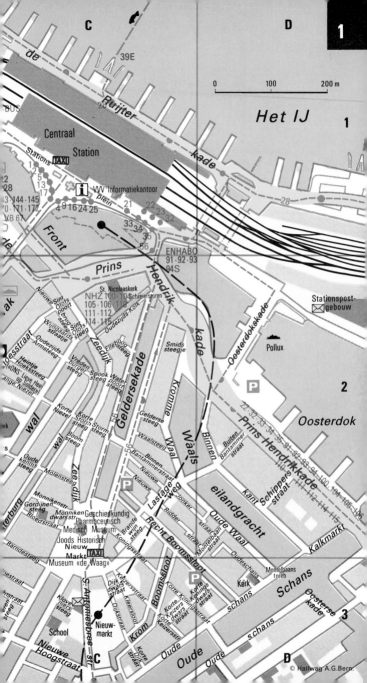

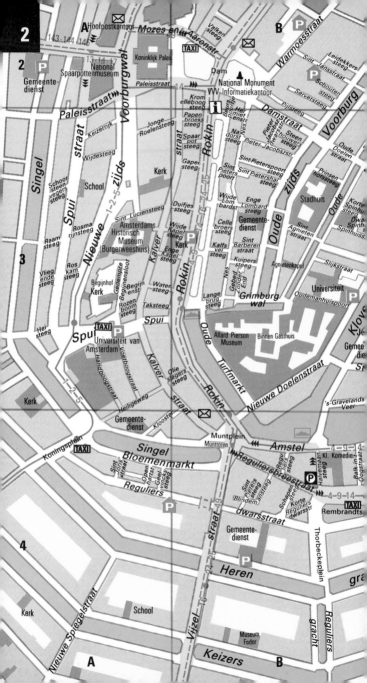

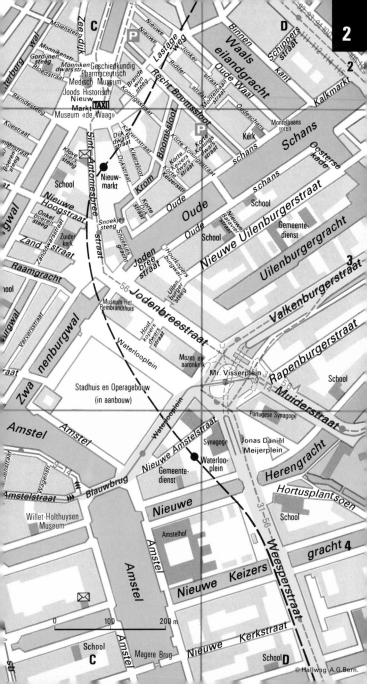

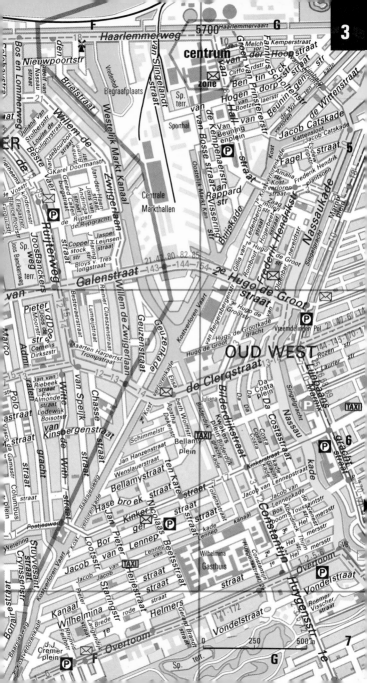

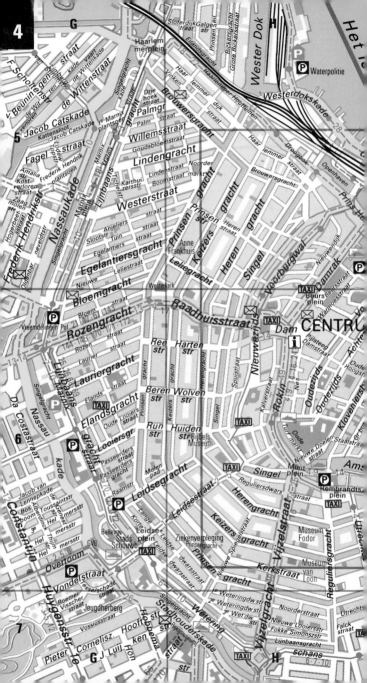

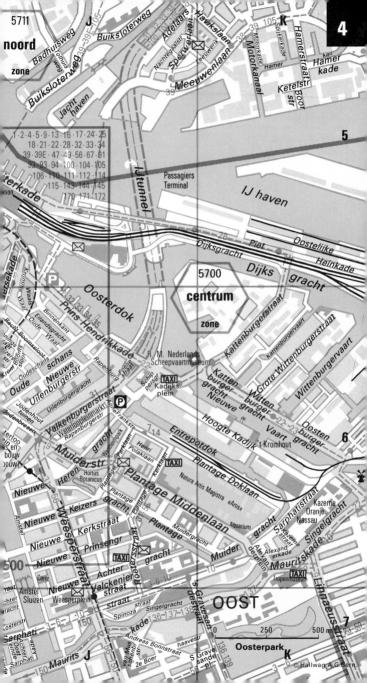

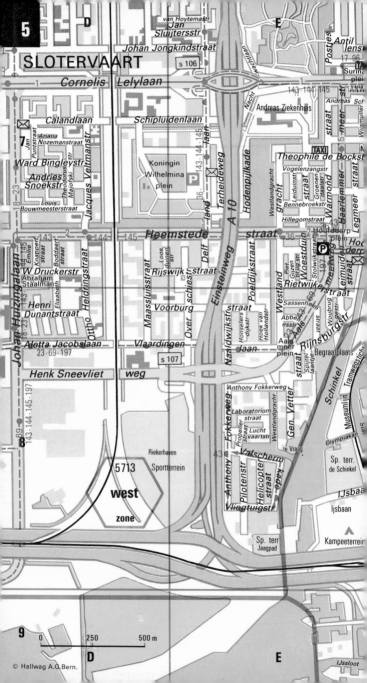

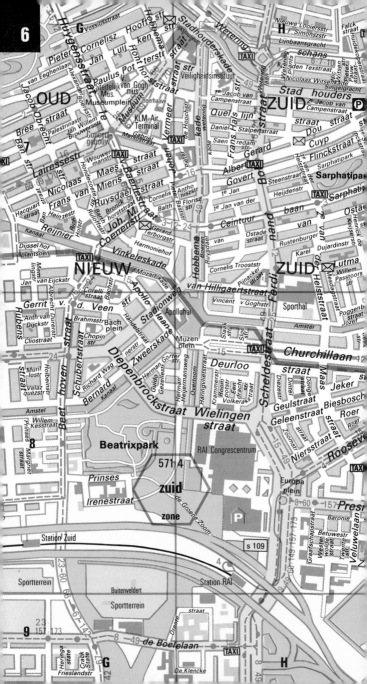

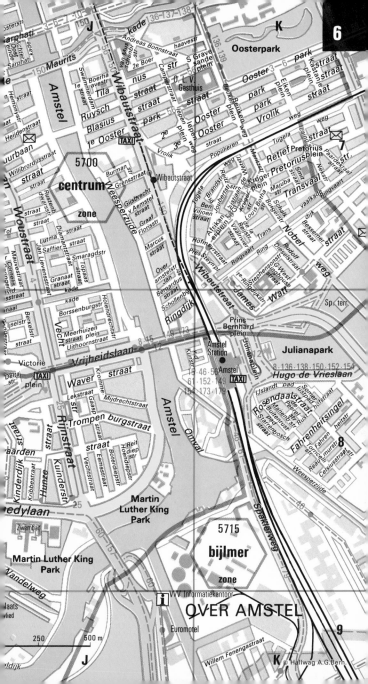

MUSEUMS AND GALLERIES

Map references (**2**B3) refer to the maps on pp. 34-45.

General information Amsterdam's major museums are closed on Mondays but are open Tuesdays-Saturdays from 1000-1700 and on Sundays and public holidays from 1300-1700. Opening days and times vary considerably in the other museums, galleries and places of historic interest. (There are about 40 lesser-known museums and public collections over and above the top three: Rijksmuseum, the Vincent van Gogh Museum, and the Stedelijk.)

Visitors are advised to double-check the opening times listed below in a local publication such as *This Week in Amsterdam*, published by the VVV in cooperation with the Cultural Information Service.

Information on all cultural aspects may be obtained from The Amsterdam Uit Buro, Leidseplein, tel: 22-90-11, or from the VVV Tourist Information Centre, Stationsplein 10, tel: 26-64-44.

Entrance fee Most museums charge a modest entrance fee which may be reduced on certain days. A museum pass, which gains admittance to over 250 museums throughout Holland, including many in the capital, may be purchased from the VVV office.

Transport mentioned below is from Centraal Station.

Allard Pierson Museum Oude Turfmarkt 127, 1012 GC (tel: 5-25-35-56). Open Tuesday-Friday 1000-1700, weekends and public holidays 1300-1700. This archaeological museum, named after a 19th-century philanthropist, is part of the University of Amsterdam. It contains articles of everyday life from various periods housed in West Asian, Cretan/Mycenaean, Cyprian, Greek, Roman and Egyptian departments. Special exhibitions are often given during the year.   **2**B3
Trams: 4, 9, 16, 24, 25.

Amstelkring Museum (Ons' Lieve Heer op Solder, Our Lord in the Attic), Oude Zijds Voorburgwal 40, 1012 GE (tel: 24-66-04). Open Monday-Saturday 1000-1700, Sundays and public holidays 1300-1700. Guided tours on request. This attic church, at the top of three small 17th-century canal houses, is the only remaining 'secret' church in Amsterdam. It was a result of the Reformation when Catholic worship in public was forbidden (1581-1795).

Church furniture and fixtures, dating from 1735, include a baroque altar with three interchangeable paintings, statues and a collection of church silver. The small 18th-century organ can still be operated by hand. Visitors can also see a well-preserved, 17th-century *Sael* (traditional Dutch living room), two kitchens, the priest's bedroom with authentic box bed and a picture gallery adorned with work by Thomas de Keyser among others. Concerts are regularly held in this miniature church and, on the first Sunday of the month, Mass is celebrated.   1C
Trams: 4, 9, 16, 24, 25, or a short walk from Centraal Station.

Amsterdam Historical Museum (Amsterdams Historisch Museum), Kalverstraat 92, 1012 PH (tel: 25-58-22). Open Tuesday-Saturday 1000-1700, Sunday and public holidays 1300-1700. Located in the former municipal orphanage (used as such from 1581 to 1960) this museum at the heart of the old city, has been beautifully restored and now contains some of Amsterdam's finest cultural heirlooms.

The public passageway, between the museum's inner court and the adjacent courtyard of the Begijnhof, is a unique street gallery of 17th-century paintings. A particularly prized painting is *The Banquet of 17 Guards* by Cornelius Anthoniszoon (1533), in which one of the guards holds the text of a love song set to music by Antoine Busnois. Visitors may listen to a recording by pushing a button.

A permanent exhibition, relating Amsterdam's history from the 13th to the 19th centuries, is on display in the girls' former quarters, while temporary exhibitions are held in what were the boys' quarters.   2A
Trams: 1, 2, 4, 5, 9, 16, 24, 25.

Anne Frank House (Anne Frankhuis), Prinsengracht 263, 1016 GV (tel: 26-45-33). Open Monday-Saturday 0900-1700, Sundays and public holidays 1000-1700. These are the rooms in which the Jewish Frank family hid from the Nazis between 1942 and 1944. It is named after one of the daughters, Anne, who, during her long 25 months here, wrote what was to become her famous diary. The family was betrayed and arrested in 1944. Anne, aged 15, died with her sister in a concentration camp in 1945. Her diary, which remains in the hideout, was first published in 1947 since when it has been translated into 50 languages and has sold some 13 million copies.   4H
Trams: 13, 17. Buses: 21, 67.

Architectuurmuseum Droogbak 1a, 1013 GE (tel: 22-02-77). Open Monday to Friday 1000-1700. This contains a variety of information on Dutch architecture dat

Our Lord in the Attic 'secret' church

Coat of arms in Historical Museum

17th-C armour in Historical Museum

Movable bookcase in the Anne Frank House

Hortus Botanicus, Plantage Middenlaan

ing from 1850 to 1940, and special exhibitions are held here during the year. **1B1**
Buses: 18, 22, or a short walk from Centraal Station.

Aviodome Schiphol Airport, 1118 AA (tel:17-36-40). Open daily 1000-1700 (Apr.-Oct.), 1000-1700 Tuesday-Sunday (Nov.-Mar.). This is the centrepiece of the National Aerospace Museum, containing more than 25 air- and spacecraft. The exhibits show the development of aviation in general and the Netherlands' role in particular.
Buses: 143, 144, 145.

Bijbels Museum (Biblical Museum), Herengracht 366, 1016 CH (tel: 24-79-49). Open Tuesday-Saturday 1000-1700, Sundays and public holidays 1300-1700. A small museum, located inside two lovely 18th-century canal houses, devoted to the Bible. It contains models, archaeological finds from the Middle East, objects relating to Jewish and Christian religious life, plus audio-visual presentations. **4H6**
Trams: 1, 2, 5.

Bilderdijkmuseum de Boelelaan 1105, 1081 HV (tel: 45-43-68). Part of the Free University. Open only by appointment. It contains manuscripts, paintings, engravings, etc., which relate to the poet Willem Bilderdijk (1756-1831).
Buses: 171, 172.

Bosmuseum Koenenkade, Amsterdamse Bos (tel: 76-21-52). Open Monday-Friday 0900-1600, weekends 1000-1700. The information centre for the Amsterdamse Bos, a large public park. It displays exhibits of the park's history.
Buses: 170, 171, 172.

Busmuseum Haarlemmermeerstation, Amstelveenseweg 264 (tel: 79-00-78). Open only by appointment. It contains about 15 historic buses built by Dutch companies.
Trams: 6, 16. Buses: 15, 23, 60.

Filmmuseum, Nederlands Paviljoen Vondelpark, Vondelpark 3, 1071 AA (tel: 83-16-46). Open Tuesday-Thursday 0900-1230 and 1330-1700. A library of film photos and posters; exhibitions and film shows are also held.
Trams: 1, 2, 5.

Fodormuseum Keizersgracht 609, 1017 DS (tel: 24-99-19). Open Tuesday-Saturday 1000-1700, Sundays and public holidays 1300-1700. Temporary exhibitions by contemporary Amsterdam artists. **2B4**
Trams: 16, 24, 25.

Fonografisch Museum Elandsgracht 111, 1016 TT (tel: 23-04-71). Open Monday-Thursday 1100-1700, Saturday 1100-1700. A unique museum, opened in 1982, containing 150 phonographs and gramophones showing the history of sound reproduction from the technology

of Edison to the compact disc. **4G6**
Trams: 7, 10, 13, 17. Buses: 26, 65, 66, 67, 69.

Geological Museum Nieuwe Prinsengracht 130, 1018 VZ (tel: 5-22-28-30). Open Monday-Friday 0900-1700. The Geological Institute of the University of Amsterdam containing a collection of stones, fossils, minerals and geological models. **4J6**
Tram: 9. Bus: 56. Metro.

Hortus Botanicus Van der Boechorststraat 8, 1081 BT (tel: 5-48-41-42). Open Monday-Friday 0900-1600. The botanical garden of the Free University lies to the south of the city. The collection of plants and ferns includes cacti and succulents, orchids and tropical plants, plus native flowers. **5F9**
Bus: 65.

Hortus Botanicus Plantage Middenlaan 2, 1018 DD (tel: 5-22-24-05). Open Monday-Friday 0900-1600, weekends and public holidays 1100-1600. The botanical garden of Amsterdam University. This garden dates back to 1682 and shelters 6000 plant species from around the world. Originally a medicinal herb garden, it is now used by the university for teaching and research. **4J6**
Tram: 9. Bus: 56. Metro.

Joods Historisch Museum (Jewish Historical Museum), Nieuwmarkt 4, 1012 CR (tel: 24-22-09). Open Tuesday-Saturday 1000-1700, Sundays and public holidays 1300-1700. Ever since the late 16th century, Jews have carved their own niche in Dutch society. At the start of the Second World War there were more than 80,000 Jews living in Amsterdam; under the occupation almost 70,000 died in concentration camps. The museum shows Jewish culture as it was, and is, in the Netherlands and includes holy objects and artistic works as well as a collection of wartime documents. **1C2**
Metro.

Kindermuseum (see p. 27.)

Koninklijk Paleis (Royal Palace), Dam (tel: 24-86-98). Open daily in summer 1230-1600. Erected in the 17th century by Jacob van Campen, the building was originally designed as the town hall. It was used as a palace (1808-10) by Louis Bonaparte, and some of his superb furniture collection is still intact and on show. The most important rooms are the huge Hall of the Burghers, the Burgomasters' Chambers and the Council Room, all of which are open to the public. The impressive Tribunal courtroom, decorated with marble sculpture, may also be visited. (See also p. 76.) **1A2**
Trams: 1, 2, 4, 5, 9, 13, 17, 24, 25. Buses 21, 67.

Madame Tussaud (see p. 27.)

Multatuli Museum Korsjespoortsteeg 20, 1015 AR (tel: 24-74-27). Open Tuesday 1000-1700 (other days by appointment). A small museum in the birthplace of the 19th-century author, Multatuli. He is best known for his novel *Max Havelaar*.   **1A1**
Trams: 1, 2, 5, 13, 17. Buses: 21, 67.

Museum Van Loon Keizersgracht 672, 1017 ET (tel: 24-52-55). Open Monday 1000-1200 and 1300-1700. The perfectly preserved Van Loon residence comprises two canal houses from the 17th/18th centuries. Of major interest in the interior is a collection of 60 portraits of the Van Loon family, including works by Van Mierevelt, Santvoort and Luttichuys. Another attraction is a medal collection coined in celebration of seven successive golden wedding anniversaries in the family, between 1621 and 1722.   **4H6**
Trams: 16, 24, 25.

Nederlands Persmuseum (Press Museum), Oude Hoogstraat 24, 1012 CE (tel: 5-25-39-08). Open Monday-Friday 1100-1700. Shows the history and development of the Dutch press since 1618 in a collection of historic, and recent, newspapers, leaflets, bric-a-brac, posters and photographs. Of particular interest are the political prints by Albert Hahn Jr. and Sr. and L.J. Jordaan.   **2B/C3**
Trams: 1, 2, 4, 5, 9, 13, 17, 24, 25.

Nederlands Scheepvaart Museum (Maritime Museum), Kattenburgerplein 1, 1018 KK (tel: 26-22-55). Open Tuesday-Saturday 1000-1700, Sundays 1300-1700. Housed in the former arsenal of the Amsterdam Admiralty built in 1656. Dutch maritime history is portrayed in ship models, paintings, charts, instruments, weapons and other related objects showing development through the ages. Three historical ships are moored at the landing stage: a sailing lugger, a steam tug and a motorized lifeboat. An appointment is needed to visit the museum's print room, department of ships' draughts or the library containing more than 60,000 volumes.   **4J6**
Buses: 22, 28.

Nederlands Theater Instituut Herengracht 166, 1016 BP (tel: 23-51-04). Open Tuesday-Friday 1000-1700, weekends and public holidays 1100-1700. The Theatre Museum is an integral part of the Institute displaying as it does the history of Dutch theatre by way of drawings and paintings, set designs and costumes. Temporary exhibitions are held here during the year. An appointment is necessary if you want to watch a video recording in the media section of the Institute.
Trams: 13, 17. Buses: 21, 67.

NINT Technical Museum Tolstraat 129, 1074 VJ (tel: 64-60-21). Open Monday-Friday 1000-1600, weekends 1300-1700. The Netherlands institute for industry and technology was founded in 1954 to stimulate interest in technical developments. The museum is housed in an old diamond cutting factory and contains a number of exhibits pertaining to photography, energy, telecommunication, computers and electronics.   **6J7**
Tram: 4.

Peter Stuyvesant Foundation Drentestraat 21, 1083 HK (tel: 5-40-69-11). Open Monday-Friday 0900-1200 and 1300-1600. Modern international paintings and sculptures are exhibited here.
Buses: 23, 65.

Rembrandthuis Jodenbreestraat 4-6, 1011 NK (tel: 24-94-86). Open Monday-Saturday 1000-1700, Sundays and public holidays 1300-1700. This is the house where Rembrandt lived between 1639 and 1659. It contains some of his drawings as well as paintings by his teacher (Pieter Lastman) and his pupils, but it is mainly devoted to Rembrandt's etchings. About 250 of them (a near-complete collection) are on display along with an explanation of the technique of etching. The house has been restored to the way it looked when he lived and worked there.   **2C3**
Tram: 9. Metro.

Rijksmuseum Stadhouderskade 42, 1071 ZD (tel: 73-21-21). Open Tuesday-Saturday 1000-1700, Sundays and public holidays 1300-1700. One of the world's greatest art museums and certainly the most important in Holland. The collection was originally housed on the upper floors of the Royal Palace before being moved to the Trippenhuis and finally to this fine home, built between 1877 and 1883 by master architect Petrus Cuypers. The art collection ranges from the 15th century to the 19th, but can be split into five distinct departments: 17th-century Dutch paintings; sculpture and decorative art; Dutch history; the Print Room and the department of Asiatic art.

If time permits a visit to only one department, then you must head for the magnificent oils on the first floor. And, if time is really short, follow the signs to the museum's most famous picture Rembrandt's *Night Watch*. But it would be a crime not to linger along the way, especially to admire the 17th-century Dutch masters: van Ruysdael's *Mill near Wijk bij Duurstede*, Jan Steen's masterpieces, works by Johannes Vermeer, Frans Hals, Albert Cuyp, plus countless others. And in Rooms 222 and 222A you will find 'the school of Rembrandt' paintings by his students and apprentices such as Govert

Flinck, Ferdinand Bol and Nicolaes Maes.

But it is Rembrandt's own work (Rooms 220-224) that is the major attraction. Here you can see his famous Self-Portrait, *Samson and Delilah* and *The Oriental Potentate*. One of his best-loved paintings is *The Jewish Bride* in glowing tones of gold and red. Another favourite is *The Syndics of the Drapers' Guild* (also known as the *Staalmeesters*). Painted quite late in his life, it was commissioned to hang in the old Cloth Hall in Amsterdam. It is a group portrait showing the Staalmeesters at a meeting, their reputation for honesty captured for eternity by the Master.

As for *Night Watch* itself (Room 224), it may not have been a night scene at all. Experts say that successive layers of protective varnish (removed after cleaning) may have darkened the canvas beyond Rembrandt's intention. Nor is the painting the original size as the small 17th-century copy displayed behind glass will show you. Whatever the history of the picture, it brought the commissioning Company of Captain Cocq and Lieutenant van Ruytenburch unforeseen and lasting fame.

Among Vermeer's masterpieces (Room 226), look out for: *A Street in Delft, A Maidservant Pouring Milk, Woman Reading a Letter* and *The Love Letter*. These are probably the greatest of the 36 works in existence.

When you leave the room which houses *Night Watch*, walk along the *Eregalerij* (Gallery of Honour) where great foreign artists have found their place. Among them hang paintings by Goya, Tintoretto and Veronese. The mezzanine floor contains Dutch paintings from 1700 to 1900.

In the sculpture and decorative art section, on the first floor, a collection of silver, textiles, furniture and glass, from the 12th to 20th centuries, includes an extensive range of Delft pottery and Dresden and Dutch porcelain. The sculpture dates back to the 14th century and includes work by Adriaen van Wesel.

On the ground floor, the modern Dutch history department illustrates the Netherlands' political and military history from the late Middle Ages to the present day while, in the six rooms of the Print Room, changing exhibitions show works taken from the Rijksmuseum's collection of over one million prints and drawings. Even on return visits you are unlikely to see the same ones twice. The Asiatic art department, also on the ground floor, contains major works of art from the Far East.

The absolute minimum time you should allow for seeing some of the work here is two hours, but it takes at least a day to do justice to this splendid museum.   **4H7**
Trams: 1, 2, 5, 16, 24, 25.

Schriftmuseum J.A. Dortmund Singe 425, 1012 WP, University Library (tel 5-25-22-66). Open Monday-Friday 1000-1300 and 1400-1630. This museum explains the history of handwriting.
Trams: 1, 2, 5.

Spaarpottenmuseum (see p.27.)   **1A2**

Stedelijk Museum Paulus Potterstraa 13, 1071 CX (tel: 73-21-66). Open Tuesday-Saturday 1000-1700, Sundays and public holidays 1300-1700. This second great Amsterdam gallery, within walking distance of the Rijksmuseum, is dedicated to modern art which has been concentrated here since 1952. Works on show cover the period from 1850 to the present day and illustrate the trends and development in painting, sculpture, drawing and engraving during that time. There are also sections on applied art and industrial design, plus posters, objects and photographs.

Here you will find a brilliant collection of modern greats: Cézanne, Monet Picasso, works by Matisse, Mondriaan Malevitch, Chagall and Dubuffet, and examples of more recent European and American art. Special exhibitions of all the visual arts are held throughout the year.

More than a museum, this is a meeting place and many Amsterdammers like to keep up to date with the art front in the modernistic restaurant on the ground floor, which opens onto a garden in fron of a small canal.   **6G7**
Trams: 2, 3, 5, 16

Tropenmuseum Linnaeusstraat 2, 1092 AD (tel: 92-49-49). Open Monday-Friday 1000-1700, weekends and public holidays 1200-1700. The Tropical Museum wa founded in 1864 in Haarlem and is now part of Amsterdam's Royal Tropical Institute. What used to be a colonial museum now emphasizes the Third World, showing how people live, where they live, their cultures and customs. Its themes are: Man and the Environment; Textiles; World Trade; Music, Dance, Theatre.   **4K6**
Tram: 9. Bus: 22.

Veiligheidsinstituut (Museum o Industrial Safety), Hobbemastraat 22 1071 ZC (tel: 73-64-14). Open Monday Friday 1000-1200 and 1400-1700. Show safety in the home and at work.   **6H7**
Trams: 16, 24, 25.

Vincent van Gogh Museum Paulu Potterstraat 7, 1071 CX (tel: 76-48-81) Open   Tuesday-Saturday   1000-1700 weekends and public holidays 1300-1700 An exciting museum opened, in 1973 alongside the Stedelijk which previousl housed a number of van Gogh's works.

The museum sets out to acquaint visi tors with van Gogh's personality throug documents, letters, literature and draw

Fodormuseum of contemporary art

Rembrandt's Night Watch, *Rijksmuseum*

Scheepvaart (Maritime) Museum

Figure of Rembrandt, Madame Tussaud's

The Rijksmuseum

Vincent van Gogh's Bedroom at Arles

ings. There are masterpieces from his 'Dutch Period', characterized by their slightly gloomy, dark atmosphere, and from the period after 1886 when the artist changed to lighter colours.

His own creative processes and the art world of his time are highlighted in both permanent and temporary exhibitions. Pictures have been chosen to show the people he mixed with, the influences he underwent and what effects they had on his work. He was also an art collector in his own right. The museum contains over 200 paintings and 500 drawings by van Gogh plus his private collections of Japanese prints, magazine illustrations and books.

Since the paintings are arranged in chronological order, a self-guided tour is easy. On the first floor, works from the 1880-1887 period are displayed, continued on the second floor up to 1890. The Paris paintings (1886-1888) form a link between the two floors. Van Gogh's drawings and private collections are located on the third floor, and on the fourth floor works by some of his contemporaries, such as Gauguin, Bernard and Monticelli, are displayed.   **6**G7
Trams: 2, 16.

Vondelmuseum Singel 425, 1012 WP, University Library (tel: 5-25-24-76). Open Monday-Friday 1000-1300 and 1400-1630. Contains books and writings about Joost van den Vondel, the 17th-century Dutch poet.
Trams: 1, 2, 5.

Werfmuseum 't Kromhout (Kromhout Shipyard), Hoogte Kadijk 147, 1018 B_ (tel: 27-67-77). Open Monday-Saturday 1000-1600, Sundays 1300-1600. A 19th-century steamboat wharf where boats are still built and repaired in the old way.
Buses: 22, 28.   **4**K6

Willet-Holthuysen Museum Herengracht 605, 1017 CE (tel: 26-42-90) Open Tuesday-Saturday 1000-1700, Sundays and public holidays 1300-1700. This handsome patrician home, now a small municipal historical museum, dates from 1687 and has a delightful 18th-century garden. It takes its name from the daughter of Pieter Gerard Holthuysen, who took over the house in 1855. She married, in 1861, Abraham Willet, a renowned collector of ceramics, silver, glass and paintings. The glass collection which, together with the house, was bequeathed to the city of Amsterdam, is of particular value. The museum opened in 1896 and affords a unique look at the lifestyle of wealthy 18th- and 19th-century patricians. Its rich furnishings, household utensils and china collections are on permanent display and there are also temporary exhibitions. **2**C4
Trams: 4, 9.

Zeiss Planetarium (see p.27.)

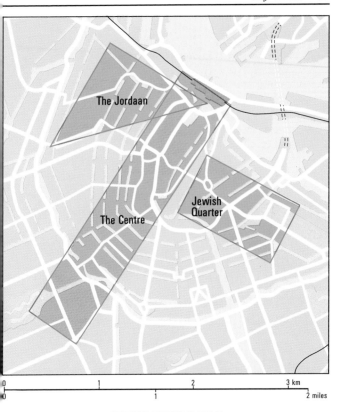

| 0 | | 1 | | 2 | | 3 km |
| 0 | | | 1 | | | 2 miles |

CITY WALKS

Jordaan Many French Huguenots settled here in the 17th century and the word may be a corruption of the French for garden, *jardin* — most of the narrow streets are named after flowers. In the last 20 years this traditional working-class area has attracted the artistic community. Today you will find many small craft studios and workshops and a lively atmosphere in the convivial corner cafés, pubs and restaurants.

Jewish Quarter The poorest settlers in the Jodenburt (Jew's quarter) lived around Waterlooplein, the more prosperous in the Plantage (Plantation). Rembrandt lived (1639-59) on Jodenbreestraat and his house can be visited today. The district was destroyed under the German occupation and, of over 80,000 Jewish Amsterdammers, almost 70,000 died in concentration camps. An eloquent memorial to that loss can be found in the former Hollandse Schouwburg (Dutch Theatre) on Plantage Middenlaan.

Centre Amsterdam is a compact city and many of the main sights are contained within the centre. This walk will take you past the Royal Palace on the Dam, to the cluster of important museums on Museumplein — Rijksmuseum, the Stedelijk and Vincent van Gogh museums — over the main canals to the floating flower market on the Singel, on to the book market and East India House, ending at the oldest and biggest church in the city, Oude Kerk.

The Jordaan

The Jordaan, or artists' quarter, is one of the oldest districts in the city. What was once a vigorous, solidly working-class area is today a very chic quarter. It is bordered by Prinsengracht to the east, Brouwersgracht to the north, Lijnbaansgracht to the west, and Looiersgracht to the south. A walk through the northern half, the most authentic and unchanged section, should take a couple of hours.

Start off in Prinsengracht at the Westerkerk (p. 72) where Rembrandt is buried. Its famous tower (85m/279ft high), symbol of the Jordaan, is just on the outskirts of the district. The statue against the church is of Anne Frank who wrote her famous diary in the house (p. 46) just around the corner, at Prinsengracht 263.

Cross the bridge over Prinsengracht and turn right. As you walk along remember to look up at the gables you pass. You will see four styles of gable in Amsterdam: the step, spout, neck and bell. The step gable, the earliest, was very popular between 1650 and 1750. The spout gable, a simplified version of the step, retained its popularity into the present century. Italian influence shows in the neck gable with its curves and raised middle bay; the bell gable was a variation of the neck. Both of these gables were popular throughout the 18th century. (At the end of the 18th century, the straight French cornice had become the fashion for the grander double-width houses.) Halfway up old buildings you will also see gablestones which were carved to portray the owner's name, place of origin or, often, his occupation.

Step gable

Spout gable

Cornice

Neck gable

Bell gable

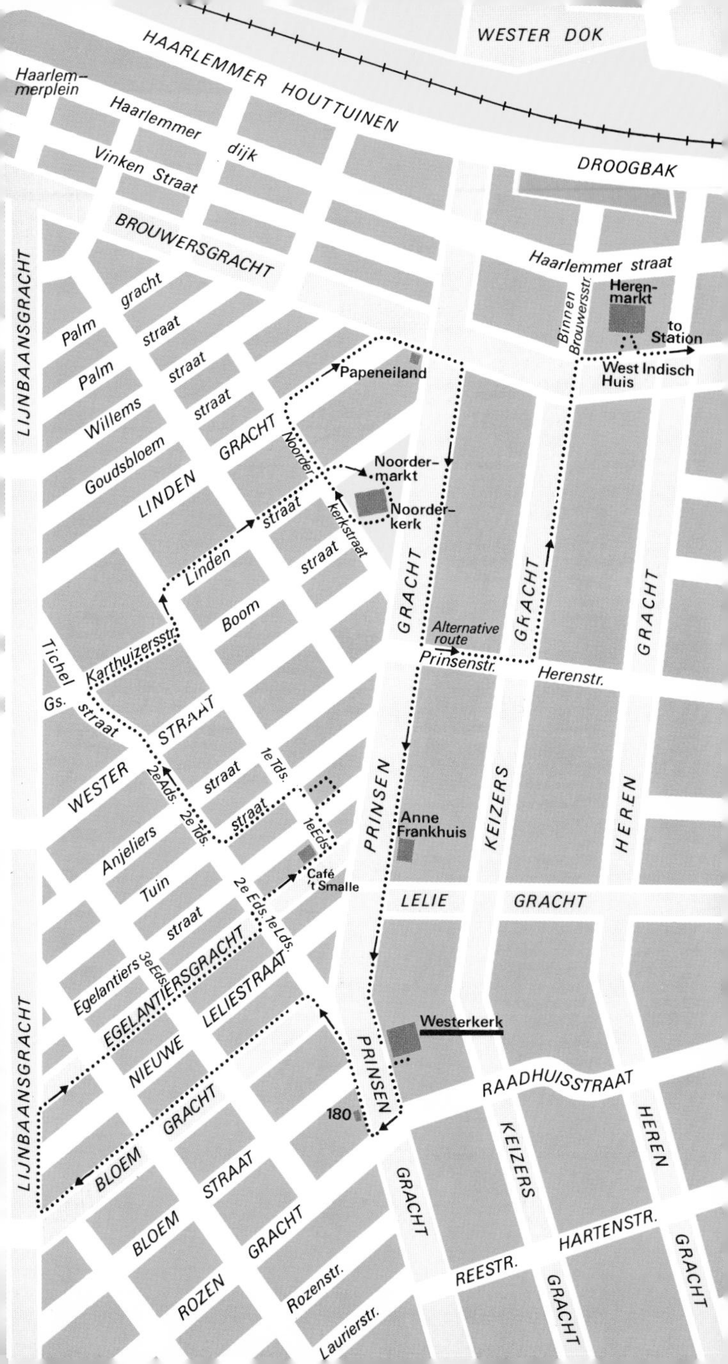

WESTER DOK

HAARLEMMER HOUTTUINEN

Haarlemmer houttuinen

Haarlemmerplein

Haarlemmer dijk

Vinken Straat

DROOGBAK

BROUWERSGRACHT

Haarlemmer straat

Heren- markt

to Station

LIJNBAANSGRACHT

Palm gracht

Palm straat

Willems straat

Goudsbloem straat

LINDEN GRACHT

Noorder

Papeneiland

Binnen Brouwersstr

West Indisch Huis

Noorder- markt

Noorder- kerk

Kerkstraat

Linden straat

Boom straat

GRACHT

GRACHT

GRACHT

Tichel Gs.

Karthuizersstr.

straat

Alternative route

Prinsenstr.

Herenstr.

WESTER STRAAT

2e Eds.

2e Eds.

straat

1e Eds.

straat

1e Eds.

PRINSEN

KEIZERS

HEREN

Anjeliers

Tuin straat

2e Eds.

1e Eds.

Café 't Smalle

Anne Frankhuis

Egelantiers straat

3e Eds.

EGELANTIERSGRACHT

LELIESTRAAT

LELIE GRACHT

NIEUWE LELIEGRACHT

Westerkerk

LIJNBAANSGRACHT

BLOEM GRACHT

PRINSEN

180

RAADHUISSTRAAT

KEIZERS

HEREN

BLOEM STRAAT

GRACHT

GRACHT

GRACHT

ROZEN GRACHT

Rozenstr.

REESTR.

HARTENSTR.

GRACHT

Laurierstr.

The gablestone was a symbol of an owner's name, place of origin or his occupation

At Prinsengracht 180 the firm, Keyzer Koffie en Thee, has been in the same location since 1839. No. 168 is an historic warehouse and note the beautiful gable, over No. 160, called 'Over Nes'.

Over the next bridge, turn left onto the Bloemgracht where the houses have particularly interesting gables. Some of the houses, such as Nos. 38 and 76, have been converted into boutiques, while the building numbered 98 dates back to 1880 and is owned by the Apostolic Missionaries. Note the neck gable at No. 116. On the other side of the canal, at numbers 83 and 85, you'll see twin gables. Next door at 87-91 are three authentic 17th-century buildings belonging to Vereniging Hendrick de Keyser. These houses are called 'Drie Hendricken' (Three Henries) because of the gablestones showing a peasant, a citizen and a sailor.

At the end of Bloemgracht turn right onto Lijnbaansgracht, and right again into Egelantiersgracht, on the odd-numbered side. Nos. 215-213 and 203-201 are four houses built in exactly the same style, all bearing the same family weapon on the gables.

Although nothing is visible from the outside, many of the 17th-century establishments contain inner courtyards. Such residences were often built to house pious lay women, the *begijnes*, who were not nuns bound by vows, but usually unmarried women with no family to care for them. There's an unobtrusive black door, next to No. 141a, which opens onto one of these courtyards, Sint Andrieshofje (1616).

If you're wondering about the hooks on some of the buildings you pass, they were used to hoist cargo or furniture as the old house doors were too narrow to give entry to bulky objects. Another feature typical of Amsterdam windows are the *spuis*, or mirrors, so angled that the person sitting several floors up could see who was at the front door below.

When you reach Eerste Leliedwarsstraat (1e Lds), make a left over the Hil-

letjes Bridge. The houses at 72-74 and 66-70 have both been restored and are owned by the Diogenes Foundation. Follow Egelantiersgracht until you reach Eerste Egelantiersdwarsstraat (1e Eds), then turn left. The Café 't Smalle on the corner is where Peter Hoppe started his distillery in 1780.

(The maze of narrow streets in this vicinity is typical of the Jordaan. Ground-floor homes along Derde Egelantiersdwarsstraat (3e Eds) show off frilly curtains backing a shelf of Delft ornaments. Tweede Egelantiersdwarsstraat (2e Eds) is another of those old-fashioned streets with charm.)

When you reach Egelantiersstraat, turn right. At No. 52 you'll notice a gablestone with a hand in writing motion on it. A schoolmaster who was a specialist in the art of writing lived here in the 17th century. (Many gablestones show what the owner's occupation was.) To the right of this house is the entrance to the Claes Claesz Hofje, where you will find four small courtyards and tiny houses. Built in 1616 for needy widows, it is now mainly occupied by students of the conservatory of music. A second exit brings you back onto Eerste Egelantiersdwarsstraat (1e Eds).

Make a right and you'll find yourself at Tuinstraat where you turn left, and maybe take a break in the small garden before continuing on to Tweede Tuindwarsstraat (2e Tds) where it's another right turn. This is one of the Jordaan's delightful shopping streets with cafés for a mid-morning coffee or orange juice. The following street, Tweede Anjeliersdwarsstraat (2e Ads), is equally pleasant.

Cross over Westerstraat, which used to be a canal until it was filled in, in 1861, and you'll have arrived at Tichelstraat. Look at the gable at No. 45 and the arms of Batavia over No. 33. At Gieterstraat (Gs) take a right turn into Karthuizersstraat. Until the end of the 16th century there used to be a convent here. The Huiszitten Weduwenhof, or widows' house, now

The French came in 1795 and imposed order by numbering the houses in every street

stands on the site. Those who donated money towards the building have their names inscribed in the pediment over the door, though the widows no longer live here.

When you get outside the court, turn right past five neck gables and then, at the end of the street, turn left and right again onto Lindenstraat where No. 34 also has a neck gable. The column neck gable at No. 19 has a stone tablet inscribed with 'D' Konig Davit', the same king also decorates Nos. 4 and 6. The barrel over the door at No. 17 shows that here they sell wines and spirits.

Now you have reached Noordermarkt where a statue commemorates the Amsterdam writer, Multatuli. Notice the gablestones at No. 21, which has a ship on it, No. 19, with a sheep, and No. 18, with a chicken. In the centre of Noordermarkt stands Noorderkerk, designed by Hendrick Staets and Hendrick de Keyser in 1620. A bird market takes place at Noordermarkt on Saturday mornings and No. 34 is a famous Jordaan café.

Walk around the church until you reach Noorderkerkstraat where at No. 14 an inscription reads *Geloof Hoop en Liefde* (faith, hope and charity). Carry on to Lindengracht where you take a right. The gablestone at No. 57 is rather interesting: it shows the year written upside down and fish swimming in the trees. It is called *'t Hcargnednil*, which in reverse spells 'Lindengracht'. The statue at the end of the street is of a character from a book by Theo Thijssen.

Aperitif time? Turn right at the Brouwersgracht and where it meets up with Prinsengracht you'll discover one of the city's oldest pubs, Papeneiland, recommended for its local atmosphere and decor. After a jenever or two, continue on right along Prinsengracht. The inscription *Nooit Weer* on the gable at No. 9 means 'never again' and shows a man at his wits' end — a sign provoked by the hassles of restoration work. All these signs tell you something about the people who lived there. At No.

35, as another example, you'll see a lone fisherman in his bobbing boat.

There are more courtyards here, too. Look through the arch into Star Court (Nos. 85-133) and, at No. 173, the Zons Hofje. If you're tired, continue to walk along Prinsengracht and you'll arrive back at Westerkerk. Otherwise, turn left on Prinsenstraat, a shopping street that leads to Keizersgracht. Over the bridge, take a left turn to admire the gables. It was here at No. 65 that the poet, P.C. Hooft, lived, though the house has since been modernized. Across the way, three more restored houses (De Groenland Pakhuizen) show ladder-shaped gables.

At the top of Keizersgracht turn right over the bridge onto Brouwersgracht (or Brewers' canal). This area is thought to be one of the most captivating in Amsterdam and is often photographed. The house on the corner, known as Binnen Brouwersstraat, is particularly attractive. Walk on and you'll arrive at Herenmarkt from where you can see the gables of West Indisch Huis. The Dutch West Indies Company's headquarters were in this building from 1623 to 1647, and it was here that it was decided to found New Amsterdam (today's New York City). In the courtyard there is a fountain and a statue of Peter Stuyvesant, one-time governor of New Amsterdam. However, the rooms have been converted into the registry office where civil marriages are performed.

Back on the Brouwersgracht, turn left. To the right of you the bow-shaped bridge is called the Melkmeisjesbrug and you can see examples of many different gables. Now you're on the Singel. Walk to the left, cross the bridge and turn right. From here, the Haarlemmersluis, you get a good view of the copper-domed Ronde Lutherse Kerk (Round Lutheran Church) where Sunday morning coffee concerts are held. You can also just about see Centraal Station which is where you should head for a bus or tram. Turn left on to Prins Hendrikkade, and the station lies to your left.

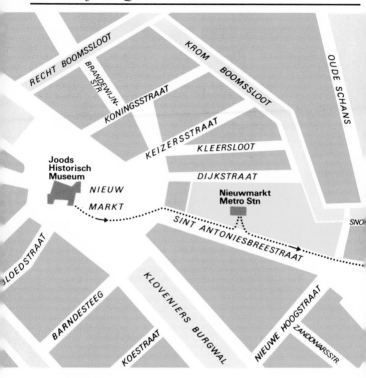

The Jewish Quarter

Although hardly anything remains of the narrow streets and alleys which once comprised the city's Jewish quarter, Amsterdam was for a long time an important Jewish centre. When the city became a major trading centre, it held an obvious attraction for Portuguese and Spanish Jews fleeing the Inquisition at the end of the 16th century. Many of the new immigrants settled in the area between Nieuwmarkt, the River Amstel and Nieuwe Herengracht. This walk will take about two and a half hours.

Start at Joods Historisch Museum (Jewish Historic Museum p. 48) in Nieuwmarkt, which gives a good introduction to the community's history, including the years of the German occupation. The objects on display reflect the social and religious life of the Jews living in Amsterdam from 1600 on. When you leave the museum, veer left and cross the road to the Nieuwmarkt metro station. When the

metro was built, a great number of houses in the Jewish quarter had to be demolished, as witnessed in the photo collection at the bottom of the stairs in the station. The picture at the end of the left-hand wall shows the house on Jodenbreestraat where Rembrandt once lived. During World War II, this same street corner was also the border of the area within which the remaining Jews were forced to stay — known as *Joodse Wijk* (Jewish district).

Back up the stairs, take the exit marked *Snoekjessteeg* which brings you onto Sint Antoniesbreestraat. In 1900, more than half the residents in this street were Jewish. Take a look at No. 69, Huis de Pinto, converted by Isac de Pinto, in 1680, into one of the district's most distinguished buildings. De Pinto, a Portuguese Jew, had great wealth as is indicated by the beautiful ceiling paintings inside and the initialled, wrought-iron window gratings. The building is now used as a public library.

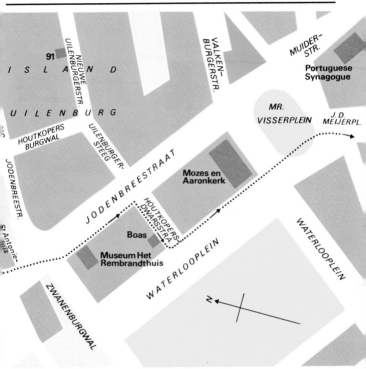

At Sint Antoniesluis there was lively trading by Jewish merchants from the 18th century on. To your left, in the distance, you can see Montelbaanstoren (Montelbaan Tower p. 76) which is supposed to be the spot where the very first Jewish refugees settled, in 1604. Cross the bridge and you're on Jodenbreestraat (Jewish Broad Street), former hub of the Jewish quarter. By 1900 almost all the inhabitants here were of Jewish origin, but the Sunday morning street markets were so popular that the ranks were always swelled by non-Jews. Rembrandthuis (p. 49), at Nos. 4-6, was the painter's home from 1639 to 1659. Now a museum, it contains almost all of Rembrandt's etchings along with paintings by his teacher and pupils.

Where Jodenbreestraat meets Houtkopersdwarsstraat, look to your left to see the remains of the Island Uilenburg. During the 16th century, this was one of the areas set aside for the poor, many of whom were East European Jews. In those days, Uilenburg comprised nothing but narrow alleys and overcrowded living quarters. The synagogue at Nieuwe Uilenburgerstraat 91 (to your left) was used by the High German Jewish community from 1766 to 1943.

Turn right into Houtkopersdwarsstraat and you'll see the Boas Factory, a diamond-polishing works which dates from 1879 when most of the skilled craftsmen were Jews. Continue along the street to Waterlooplein. This used to be an island called 'Vloyenburg' which regularly flooded at times of high water. The canals were filled in and it was renamed Waterlooplein in 1883. It became internationally known for its flea market (since relocated in Valkenburgerstraat due to the construction of a new town hall and opera house on Waterlooplein).

This was the area of clandestine synagogues in the 17th century. Amsterdam's reputation for tolerance meant that no-

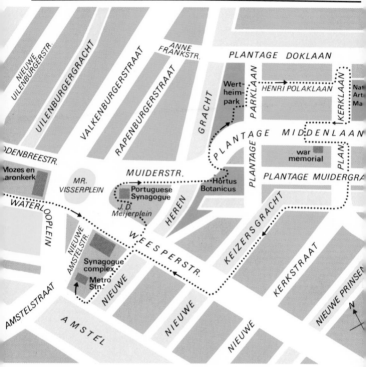

one was persecuted because of his religious beliefs. It did not mean freedom to hold religious services openly. The Jews held their services in private homes until 1630 when their places of worship became legal. In 1639 the first official Portuguese Synagogue, the Talmud Tora, was built.

The Catholics in the neighbourhood had the same problem, and they too had to find secret worshipping places. Mozes en Aaronkerk (Moses and Aaron Church) was once a clandestine Catholic church. It stands close to the spot where the philosopher, Spinoza, is believed to have been born (Waterlooplein 41) in 1632. Today the church serves as a youth centre, though services are still held here on Sunday mornings.

Walk past the church and cross the street. On the other side is the Huiszittenhuis where free food and peat were once given to the poor. The three warehouses to the right date from 1610. You have now reached Mr. Visserplein where, to the right, stands the Synagogue complex of the High German Jews, comprising four

synagogues the first of which was built in 1670. Together these form the most important Jewish monument in Europe: the 'small' German Synagogue (1670) stands on the corner of Nieuwe Amstelstraat, next to it is the Drittsjoel, or third synagogue (1700), behind it is the Obbene Sjoel, or second synagogue (1686) and left of it stands the New Synagogue (1752), largest of the four. When the complex has been completely restored, it will house the Jewish Historical Museum.

Across Weesperstraat, in the middle of Jonas Daniël Meijerplein, stands De Dokwerker (dockworker) statue, a monument to the strike of 1941 when Amsterdammers proclaimed solidarity with the persecuted Jews.

Now you are in front of the Portuguese Synagogue which, on completion in 1675, was the world's largest. The architect, Elias Bouman, influenced by the Temple of Solomon, designed the building to face towards Jerusalem. The synagogue whose 17th-century interior is still intact is open daily 1000-1300 (closed Saturdays and

Rembrandt's house on Jodenbreestraat

Jewish Historical Museum in the Waag

Jewish holidays). The Hebrew inscription above the entrance reads 'And I in Your great love — shall come unto Your house'. The famed Ets Haim (Tree of Life) library adjoins the synagogue. To appreciate how tall the building is, walk round it via Mr. Visserplein, turning right into Muiderstraat. Note the pelican sign above the gateway in the wall — the symbol of love, and of the Portuguese Jews in Amsterdam.

To reach the fringe of the Jewish quarter, walk along Muiderstraat and cross the Hortusbrug into Plantage Middenlaan. This district attracted the more prosperous Jews towards the end of the 19th century and, by 1924, half the population was Jewish. It is here in the Plantage that you can visit Hortus Botanicus gardens (p. 48) before crossing over to the Wertheimpark. Abraham Carel Wertheim was a noted 19th-century banker, philanthropist and chairman of the Jewish Religious Community. A monument dedicated to him stands in the middle of this park.

At Plantage Parklaan, swing left, then right into Henri Polaklaan where No. 10 is the Algemene Nederlandse Diamantbewerkers Bond (General Dutch Diamond Workers League). Designed by the architect Berlage, in 1900, it looks rather like a fortress — a palace for proles rather than patricians. Opposite stands the former Portuguese-Israelite Hospital (1916).

When you come to the Natura Artis Magistra zoo (p. 27), at the end of Henri Polaklaan, turn left into Plantage Kerklaan and see the front of the Plancius building at No. 61, once a centre for Jewish choral societies. This neighbourhood used to be the location of numerous concert halls and theatres, such as the Hollandse Schouwburg (Dutch Theatre) at 24 Plantage Middenlaan. Prior to 1942 all the well-known Jewish artists performed here. The Nazis used the theatre building as a transit centre for arrested Jews and after the war this site became an eloquent memorial with an ever-burning lamp.

Turn back to Plantage Kerklaan and turn right crossing the bridge at Nieuwe Keizersgracht. On the corner stand the Lutherhuis (1856) and the Lutherse Oude Mannen en Vrouwenhuis (1772), both built for Lutheran pensioners. At Nieuwe Keizersgracht 94, Occo's Hofje was built in 1774 for needy Roman Catholics. The reason for the number of 18th-century poorhouses in this district east of the Amstel was because at that time private land sales were going badly and the city administration made land available for buildings to house the needy and elderly.

Crossing Weesperstraat, turn right into the small park. You will pass a monument on your left, dedicated in 1947 'To the protectors of Dutch Jewry in the years of occupation'.

The Vaz Diazbrug (bridge) is named after a Portuguese-Jewish journalist. After crossing it, turn left onto Nieuwe Herengracht, sometimes referred to as 'Jewish Herengracht' because many wealthy Jewish immigrants settled along it. The River Amstel is reckoned to be the boundary of the Jewish quarter. Continue right alongside the river to Waterlooplein where a metro will take you back to Nieuwmarkt.

A Walk round the Centre

This walk starts out at Stationsplein but you might like to fortify yourself first with a coffee in the Koffiehuis across from Centraal Station. The original coffee house was built overlooking the water in 1911 and became a popular rendezvous. Torn down to make way for the metro, it was rebuilt after much protest, and reopened in 1981. Centraal Station, a noted city landmark, was built by P.J.H. Cuypers between 1884 and 1889 on an artificial island. This walk will take about three and a half hours.

After coffee, turn left over the bridge towards the Victoria Hotel and walk along the Damrak, a busy, cosmopolitan shopping street. On the other side stands the Koopmansbeurs (Stock Exchange p. 76) built by Berlage. Further up the side you're walking on is a statue of a man holding a newspaper, known as *Beursmannetje,* donated by the Dutch Financial Times. Opposite, rollerskaters frequent Beursplein which also supports a modern Jonah and the Whale sculpture. Next to the square is Amsterdam's largest and most famous department store, the Bijenkorf (Beehive).

The Damrak and its parallel streets are at the heart of the oldest section of the city. When the Damrak was part of the River Amstel, ships used to load and unload salt cargo at the Zoutsteeg. Turn right into Zoutsteeg, a narrow street full of small shops and restaurants and, after crossing Nieuwendijk, you come to a similar street, called Gravenstraat.

Drop in at No. 2, the Café De Wenteltrap, which has a unique collection of caps above the bar, or into the 17th-century tasting house, De Drie Fleschjes (The Three Bottles) at No. 18. From this spot on Gravenstraat you can see the chancel of the Nieuwe Kerk (New Church), originally built in the 15th and 16th centuries. Look both sides of the porch and you'll see Amsterdam's (possibly Europe's) smallest shops, only 8 sq.m/9.5sq.yd. Bear left past these shops, noting the pear-shaped tower decorations of the city's main post office on the other side of Nieuwe Zijds Voorburgwal. (The name of this major street means 'new side of the city moat', and it runs parallel to Damrak. On the other side of the Damrak is Oude Zijds Voorburgwal, or 'old side of the moat'.)

You can see the Royal Palace in front of you so you're nearly at Amsterdam's most central square. Take Mozes en Aaronstraat to the left and you've arrived at the Dam. Dam Square (p.73) is the most popular meeting point in the city and sightseeing canal boats leave from here. It's worth checking opening hours (with the VVV)

for a tour of the interior of the Royal Palace (p. 76), built originally as a town hall between 1648 and 1655 in the Golden Age. And it is worth going into Nieuwe Kerk (p. 71) which, since 1814, has been used for coronations. The National Monument (p. 76) here was built in 1956 in memory of those who died in World War II.

Walking past the palace, cross the street to Kalverstraat, a busy pedestrian shopping street. No. 92 used to be an orphanage (from 1581 to 1960). Today it is the Amsterdams Historisch Museum (Historical Museum p. 46). You can visit the courtyards and the Schuttersgalerij, where 17th-century paintings are exhibited in the street, without having to go right through the museum, if you wish.

Between Nos. 130 and 132 on Kalverstraat, there's a tiny passage, the Begijnensteeg. Go down it, enter the gate at the end and be prepared for a surprise — an 18th-century oasis, the Begijnhof (p. 70) is a perfectly preserved cluster of homes built by the socially conscious and wealthy for Amsterdam's poor. This is the city's best-known *hofje* (charity-built almshouse for the deserving poor) though there are many others scattered throughout Amsterdam. In the centre of the square you'll see a Presbyterian church and, opposite, a Roman Catholic one. No. 34 is the oldest wooden house remaining in the city. It dates from 1475.

Walk through the porch between Nos. 37 and 38 onto the Spui. The building opposite is the main building of the University of Amsterdam while the statue Het Lieverdje (Little Darling) to your right typifies an Amsterdam street urchin — boisterous but essentially good at heart.

To cross the Singel, on your right, take the Heisteeg, a small street just right of the café Hoppe. Up until the 17th century, the Singel served as a rampart. Now walk through the Wijde Heisteeg where at No. 4 there's a signpost of someone yawning (traditional sign of the apothecary). When you reach the bridge crossing the Herengracht, look left for one of the best city views. From here you can see a multitude of different gables and, in the distance, the Leidsegracht.

Turn left after the bridge to pass the Bijbels Museum (Biblical Museum p. 48) at No. 366. No. 380 has an abundance of sculpture and was built in the 19th century for a rich tobacco planter. The houses 390-392 were built in 1665 and have neck gables. Continue to follow the Herengracht, over the Leidsegracht and Leidsestraat, to reach what is called the 'Golden Bend' of the Herengracht, notable for its expensive and splendid houses built on two costly lots instead of the more usual one.

At this bend, turn into Nieuwe Spiegelstraat, the antique quarter. Don't expect to find junk along here or in the side streets, but there are plenty of old books, prints, fine furniture and porcelain. The street leads you to the Rijksmuseum (p. 49), designed by P.J.H. Cuypers in 1885. You may well want to leave a visit to this major Dutch museum until another time — if so, use the passage underneath to reach Museumplein. Cross the street and walk on towards the Concertgebouw (p. 73). On the way you'll pass the Vincent van Gogh Museum (p. 50). Beyond the gardens of the Stedelijk Museum (p. 50), make a right into van Baerlestraat. Cross Paulus Potterstraat, Jan Luijkenstraat and turn into the city's most elegant and pricey shopping street, P.C. Hooftstraat. This is where you'll find couturier labels and the finest of foods. At Hobbemastraat, turn left and left again onto the Stadhouderskade.

The entrance to Vondel Park is also on your left but a visit there might take up more time than you have. Cross over instead and walk past the Lido towards Leidseplein, a popular nightlife area, bordered by cafés and clubs. Look to the right of the American Hotel — that's the Stadsschouwburg (Municipal Theatre) where ballet, opera and other performances take place. Continue on past the large terrace that doubles as an ice-skating rink in winter, through Leidsestraat, passing the three main canals: Prinsengracht, Keizersgracht and Herengracht, until you reach Koningsplein.

Turn right on to the Singel — this is the spot where the Bloemenmarkt (floating market) is situated. The flowers are fabulous and very inexpensive. At the end of the market is the Muntplein (p. 76) with its Munttoren (Mint Tower, 1620) right in the middle. This square is a very wide bridge built across the River Amstel. Cross it and turn left into Rokin; across the river, on Oude Turfmarkt, is the Allard Pierson Museum (p. 46). By Arti's, at No. 112, cross over and pass the statue of Queen Wilhelmina before walking into Langebrugsteeg, passing the Nes to your left.

Years ago, Langebrugsteeg was full of theatres, bars and brothels. Then the tobacco industry took up occupation, but now entertainments are beginning to return. By contrast, there also used to be numerous convents in the area which is why the alley on the left is called 'Gebed Zonder End' (prayer without end). Someone could always be heard mumbling their prayers here. Following the Grimburgwal, you cross both the Oude Zijds Voorburgwal and the Oude Zijds Achterburgwal.

Between these canals is a house called Huis aan de Drie Grachten (house on the three canals).

On the far side of Oude Zijds Achterburgwal, turn into the Oudemanhuispoort where during the week a book market is held. The books are mainly second-hand or antique and could be well worth browsing. The Oudemanhuis (old man's home) is being used by the University of Amsterdam — walk through the courtyard and turn into Kloveniersburgwal.

The lovely canal house at No.95, Poppenhuis, was named after the 1642 owner. Take a look, too, at the Oost Indisch Huis (East India House) of 1606, and its courtyard, before turning left into Oude Hoogstraat. Via Oude Doelenstraat you reach Oude Zijds Voorburgwal where you cross the bridge and turn right. There's a portrait of the sea hero, Admiral Tromp, at No. 136, though he never lived here and, in front of you, Oude Kerk (Old Church). Building of this Late Gothic church began in 1300. It was known as St Nicolaaskerk until 1578. Maximilian of Austria and his son, Philip, were among those who donated money towards the church's construction, and their coat of arms can be seen in the south porch. Do take a look inside the church — its inscribed Holy Grail dates from 1530. You can walk around the church onto the Oudekerksplein.

To get back to where you started from is only a little way now: walk through Enge Kerksteeg and turn right onto Warmoesstraat. Turn left into Oudebrugsteeg and the building at the end of this street is the Stock Exchange, back on the Damrak.

Leidsegracht

Allard Pierson Museum

The House on the Three Canals

The main street of Vijzelstraat leading to the city centre

CITY SIGHTS

Map references (**2**A3) refer to the maps on pp. 34-45.

The heart of Amsterdam, Centrum, contains all the major sights, monuments and museums. Your first, broad look at the city is best taken from a canal boat, but the centre should really be explored on foot. With map in hand, you're unlikely to get lost. Thanks to the 17th-century burghers who laid out this city of streets and canals, there is a discernible pattern: a wide U-shape of canals split down the middle by the continuous main streets of Damrak, Rokin, Vijzelstraat.

The inner city is contained by four main concentric canals, *grachten*. (Any name ending in 'gracht' is bound to be a canal, bordered on either side by a narrow road and crossed by bridges. Only in a few instances, such as the Rozengracht, has a former canal been completely filled in to form one road.)

The Singel First of the four main canals, the Singel (meaning moat, or girdle) is the innermost ring and was once the fortified boundary of the city. It starts just outside the old city and sweeps round from the west side of Centraal Station to the Muntplein (Mint Square). It is best known today for its floating flower market (Bloemenmarkt), open daily.

Herengracht Once the merchants had built their houses along the Singel, they expanded outwards and the Herengracht, Gentlemen's Canal, was built at the start of the 17th century. This was *the* address in the Golden Age when wealthy merchants competed to build the widest houses with ornate gables along the stretch known as the Golden Bend, between Leidsestraat and Vijzelstraat. The houses are still here, though today they are mainly commercial premises.

Keizersgracht The Emperor's (Maximilian I of Austria) Canal is the third concentric ring and, although the houses here were never as impressive as those on Herengracht, they are still fine examples of middle-class homes in the 17th and 18th centuries. The finest houses lie between Westermarkt and Vijzelstraat.

Prinsengracht The Princes' Canal, last of the four main canals, contains smaller houses, lots of little cafés and many 17th-century warehouses still in use today.

Keizersgracht

Where Prinsengracht meets Brouwersgracht

Prison bridge on the Singel

Houses along Herengracht

Begijnhof   2A3

The Beguine Court is often missed by visitors, located as it is behind closed doors off the bustle of Kalverstraat. It is, however, one of Holland's most delightful *hofjes* (small housing developments built for the poor by socially-aware, rich families in the 16th and 17th centuries).

Little more than a quadrangle of grass surrounded by 17th- and 18th-century homes (still housing the elderly poor), the courtyard has a Roman Catholic church and a Presbyterian church.

Canal Houses

It would be impossible to list all the many beautiful and architecturally interesting merchants' houses lining Amsterdam's canals. Originally, these narrow houses were warehouse, office and home in one. In those days tax was levied according to canal frontage. Once a merchant became rich he could afford to build a statelier, double-width house, called a *herenhuis*.

The foundations of canal houses had to be laid deep enough to accommodate storage cellars, while the ground floor had to be raised high enough to stay free of rising damp. That is why the ground floor is above street level and is generally reached by a flight of steps. Many canal houses lean over the street. This was to keep the rain off and also to allow cargo and furniture to be hoisted up to the top floors.

Gables have made Amsterdam photographically renowned. The step gable appeared first, around 1600, and lasted well into the 17th century when Hendrick de Keyser was one of the most influential architects. Houses with oval windows under the gable are likely to have been built between 1630 and 1680.

Modest houses often featured the simple spout gable throughout most of the 17th century, while the neck gable evolved from the step, about 1650, when Jacob van Campen introduced the Italian Classical style. The bell gable was a variation of the neck gable and these two types of gable vied for fashionability in the 18th century.

From the second half of the 17th and throughout the 18th centuries, the flat cornice made its appearance, particularly on the double-width houses. Such cornices often boasted an elaborate crest to set off their coats of arms. To see the best of the 17th-century canal houses, look to the lower numbers along the canals towards the central Dam.

(See gables on p. 54.)

Churches

Amsterdam is a city of churches of all denominations. It has always been a tolerant city, welcoming the Portuguese and Spanish Jews and allowing them to build their synagogues, receiving the Huguenots when they were expelled from France, and taking in many other refugees seeking religious freedom and shelter. At a time of constant religious controversy, Protestants, Catholics, Jews and other minorities lived in peaceful harmony in the Dutch capital.

Nieuwe Kerk (New Church) Next to the Royal Palace on the Dam. Well, it was *new* early in the 15th century. Since 1814 it has been many Dutch coronations, including that of Queen Beatrix in 1980. Note its late Gothic chancel and the two tiny shops (probably Europe's smallest) built into the church walls. Several of the nation's distinguished people are buried in this church. **1A/B2**

Noorderkerk (North Church) On Noordermarkt. This is a lovely 17th-century Roman Catholic church, around which a market takes place — textiles on Monday mornings and birds on Saturday mornings. **4H5**

Oude Kerk (Old Church) On Oudekerksplein. The oldest and biggest church in the city dates back to the 14th century and, bizarrely, stands on the fringe of the red-light district. **1C2**

Portuguese Synagogue Jonas Daniël Meijerplein. At the heart of the former Jewish quarter, this magnificent synagogue was built by Sephardic Jews, descendants of the refugees who had fled the Inquisition in Spain and Portugal. When it was completed in 1675, it was the world's largest Jewish place of prayer. The architect, Elias Bouman, borrowed from drawings of Solomon's Temple when he was designing the synagogue. The 17th-century interior is still intact and is open to

Oude Kerk, oldest church in the city

public view 1000-1300 daily (closed Saturdays and Jewish holidays).

In front of the synagogue is the impressive statue, De Dokwerker (dockworker) a monument, by Mari Andriessen, commemorating the strike, on 25 February 1941, called to proclaim solidarity with the persecuted Jews. The memory of this strike is observed annually in a march past the statue.   **2D4**

Westerkerk (West Church) On the Prinsengracht, a few steps from the Anne Frank House. Built between 1620 and 1630 to the architectural designs of Hendrick de Keyser, Westerkerk's most distinctive feature is the ornate crown which tops its steeple. In summer (1400-1700 hrs) visitors may climb to the top of this tower, the city's highest; the observation deck is 85 m/279 ft above the ground. Rembrandt is buried in Westerkerk and Princess (now Queen) Beatrix was married here in 1966.   **4G5**

Zuiderkerk (South Church) Zandstraat. This Church was built between 1603 and 1611 by Hendrick de Keyser. Visitors pass through the Zuiderkerkhof gateway (p. 80) into the churchyard and look up at what is considered by many to be Amsterdam's most beautiful tower, the Zuidertoren, added in 1614.   **2C3**

Medieval window in Nieuwe Kerk

Tower of Westerkerk

Concertgebouw

Concertgebouw 6G7

On Museumplein. One of the world's finest concert halls, it is renowned for its acoustics. The Concertgebouw Orchestra season runs from mid-September to March, though the orchestra may also be heard during the Holland Festival, in June, and on some additional weeks during the year.

The concert hall opened in 1888 with the orchestra under the direction of Willem Kes who established the basis of its fine reputation. Kes was followed by Willem Mengelberg who was with the Concertgebouw Orchestra for half a century, developing it into one of the best in the world. After the last war Eduard van Beinum continued the great tradition. Such were the achievements of these men that composers such as Richard Strauss dedicated works to the Concertgebouw. (See also p. 23.)

Dam Square 1B2

The city began here some 800 years ago. There are a number of important buildings on or near this square, including the Royal Palace (p. 76) and Nieuwe Kerk (New Church, p. 71), as well as hotels such as the Krasnapolsky (affectionately called the 'Kras'), shops and cafés. The Dam is always full of life and one of the most popular meeting places in town.

Damrak 28-30 1B2

This building used to house the offices of the life assurance company, De Utrecht, and is noted for the five sculptures in front of it. The figures were created by Mendes da Costa, in 1905, and they show: *de Waakzaamheid* (Vigilance — the woman with the dog), *de Wisselvalligheid der tijden* (the Vicissitudes of the Ages — the woman with the hourglass with a chameleon on it), *de Wijsheid het kwaad bedwingend* (Wisdom subduing Evil), *de Spaarzaamheid* (Thrift — the woman with a money box), and *de Beschermende Liefde* (the Love that Protects). Above the entrance, in front of the Wheel of Fortune, the bronze figure is *de Weduwe* (the Widow).

De Drie Fleschjes 1A/B2

Gravenstraat 18. 'The Three Bottles' is one of Amsterdam's oldest tasting houses and is worth seeing in its own right, whether or not you decide to try one of the many liqueurs and gins on sale here. It is a small tavern with only a couple of chairs and is best visited outside of crowded *borreltje* (small drink) time around 1700 hours.

Magere Brug, the 'Skinny Bridge'

Magere Brug by night

In the Leidseplein

Sightseeing boats on Damrak

Europaplein   6H8
Lying to the south of the city, this square is famous for the RAI exhibition and conference centre, one of the largest in the world.

Heineken's Brewery   6H7
Stadhouderskade 78, where it meets Ferdinand Bolstraat. Holland is renowned for its beer and Heineken provide free tours (and samples) on a first-come, first-served basis Mon.-Fri. 1000-1130. The informative guided tour covers the complete brewing process, including the bottling works and, afterwards, there are generous servings of the product in the beer hall.

Het Lieverdje   2A3
On the Spui, a square just off Nieuwe Zijds Voorburgwal. Called affectionately 'Little Darling', this bronze statue of an urchin embodies the spirit of all Amsterdam street urchins — mischievous yet ready to be helpful. It was sculpted by Carel Kneulman and unveiled on the Spui in 1960.

Kloveniersburgwal 26   2C3
Close to Nieuwmarkt, Amsterdam's narrowest house (only 2.5 m/8 ft wide) was built by a wealthy 17th-century merchant for his coachman who had been heard saying, 'I'd be happy to have a house just as wide as your front door'.

Koopmansbeurs   1B2
Damrak. The Stock Exchange was built by the architect Berlage between 1898 and 1903. On the corner are statues of Jan Pietersen Coen, founder of what is now Jakarta, and Gijsbrecht van Aemstel, the subject of a play by Joost van den Vondel, poet and playwright of the Dutch Renaissance.

Leidseplein   4G6
The word *plein* means square. Located at the end of Leidsestraat, just at the edge of the inner city, Leidseplein is a popular place of entertainment. Here you'll find lively cafés, inexpensive sandwich shops, cabaret and other amusements. Here, too, is the Stadsschouwburg, or Municipal Theatre.

Leprozenpoortje   2C3
Along Snoekjesgracht (which turns into St Antoniesluis) at the top of the steps. A gateway made around 1610 in Hendrick de Keyser's workshop. It was the entrance to a nursing home for lepers. A male and female leper are depicted on either side of the coat of arms of Amsterdam.

Magere Brug   2C4
Nieuwe Kerkstraat. Spanning the River Amstel, the 'Skinny Bridge' is much photographed. It is a white wooden drawbridge linked by handsome stone arches to either river bank, and opens when necessary to allow the passage of barge traffic.

Montelbaanstoren   1D3
Close to the port, on the Oude Schans canal. A remnant of the medieval city wall, the wooden spire was added to the tower in 1606 by the architect and sculptor, Hendrick de Keyser.

Muiderpoort   4K6
On Mauritskade, where the bridge crosses over Singelgracht to Plantage Middenlaan. Built in 1771. It was through this gateway that Napoleon Bonaparte entered the city at the end of the 18th century.

Muntplein   2B4
Mint Square, adjoining the floating flower market, is a wide bridge crossing the Singel canal. Best known for the Munttoren (Mint Tower) with its 17th-century carillon which chimes out a traditional Dutch tune every half hour. During a war in the 17th century, the city minted its money for a time in this building.

Museumplein   6G7
This square is so named because it is Amsterdam's cultural hub. Bordered by lawns and trees, it is the site of three of Europe's major museums: the Rijksmuseum, Vincent van Gogh Museum and Stedelijkmuseum (see Museums). It is also the site of the Concertgebouw, the city's notable concert hall (p. 73).

National Monument   1B2
This white stone column in the middle of Dam Square is dedicated to the Dutchmen who died during World War II. It was built by public subscription and contains twelve urns filled with soil from Holland's eleven provinces, the twelfth is filled with soil from Indonesia.

Rembrandtsplein   2B4
Located one block from Muntplein, this square with its grassy garden centre is one of Amsterdam's nightlife meccas (together with adjoining Thorbeckeplein). All round the square are clubs, cafés, cinemas, pubs, discos and hotels.

Royal Palace
(Koninklijk Paleis)   1A2
Dam Square. Built as the town hall in the 17th century by the master builder, Jacob van Campen. At the time its dimensions broke several records. The Burgerzaal (Hall of the Burghers) in the centre of the

palace, for example, was larger than any other existing room, and higher: 28m/93ft from floor to beautifully painted ceiling. The design of the building was inspired by the architecture of Ancient Rome. Work started in 1648 and was completed in 1655.

The carillon is the work of the famous bell founders of Lotharing, François and Pierre Hemony. Influenced by Palladio, van Campen imported Irish sandstone for his palatial town hall. Above the entrance, on top of a vast tympanum, stands the statue of the Virgin of Peace gazing down on the Dam. The building still rests on most of the 13,659 original wooden piles which served as its foundation.

The interior represents the universe. In the Burgerzaal, celestial and terrestrial globes are depicted in the marble inlaid floor. Sculpted figures of the elements fill the arches at either end of the room and the planets are portrayed in the surrounding galleries. Artus Quellinus, who was commissioned to create the sculptures, brought ten apprentices with him from South Holland.

Marble-finished pillars support the rooms and corridors and the interior is filled with enormous paintings and statues. Oddly enough, when Rembrandt was commissioned to do a painting for the town hall, his first work, *Portrait of a Roman Consul*, was not accepted and has since disappeared. His second, *The Oath of Claudius Civilis*, decorated a gallery for only a year before being taken down, and it was then cut into small pieces by Rembrandt himself. The paintings of Rembrandt's pupils, Ferdinand Bol and Govert Flinck, however, were accepted and are still on view today. In the Schepenzaal you can see the painting of *Moses descending from Mount Sinai with the Tablet of Stone* by Bol.

Originally the town hall also housed the law court where offenders were chained to the vaults in the walls while they awaited trial. One could at least say it was an impressive place in which to be detained.

The French occupied Amsterdam in 1795 and Louis Bonaparte was the first to use this building as a palace, in 1808. On the return of the House of Orange in 1813, Amsterdam took back its town hall and loaned it to the royal house. In the 1930s the state paid ten million guilders for the ownership. Today the palace is used for official receptions, state visits, gala dinners, cultural activities and exhibitions, often attended by the royal family (who prefer to live most of the year in their palace in The Hague).

The main entrance is scarcely noticeable and not in keeping with the size of the building. Behind the gallery with its seven

National Monument with the Royal Palace in the background

The flea market on Waterlooplein has moved across the road to Valkenburgerstraat

Munttoren (Mint Tower) on Muntplein

arches representing the number of provinces originally comprising the Netherlands, are two small doors. They lead to the vestibules which open out onto the staircases. Between the stairs, the white marble-lined room was where the law court sat.

Central heating was installed in 1938 and the plumbing was modernized. Full-scale restoration was completed in 1966 and now the palace is open to the public in the summer; daily 1230-1600 (for information tel: 24-86-98).

Scheepvaarthuis   1D2

On the corner of Prins Hendrikkade and Binnenkant. Built by J. M. van der Mey, between 1912 and 1916, as the offices of six Amsterdam shipping companies. Some of the sculpture is by the municipal sculptor, Hildo Krop (1884-1970). Here you will see a ship with a figure of Neptune at its prow, symbolizing trade and, on the walls, many nautical emblems.

Schreierstoren   1C2

The 'Tower of Tears' is located near the harbour, close to Centraal Station. Story has it that from here Amsterdam's seafarers set sail after bidding goodbye to weeping families. They also say it was from this tower, in 1609, that Henry Hudson set sail on his historic voyage to Nieuwe Amsterdam, or what is now New York City.

Stationsplein   1C1

Stationsplein is important as a key arrival and departure point. Centraal Station stands where the port used to be, built on reclaimed land at the edge of the harbour. Buses and trams go from here to almost all parts of the city and it is also a departure point for sightseeing canal boats.

Stedelijk Museum Sculpture Garden   6G7

Museumplein. In front of the museum's new wing there are a number of interesting sculptures: a reclining figure by Henry Moore (1957), *Huiselijke Zorgen* (Domestic Concerns) by Rik Wouters (1913), *Ontwakend Afrika* (Africa Awakening) by Wessel Couzijn (1961), *Lanleff* by Henri Etienne Martin (1961) and a stainless steel *Kubus* by Andre Volten (1970).

The most dramatic sculpture in the garden is the 12m/40ft high *Sight Point* by Richard Serra. Among the other sculptures here are *Large Squatting Woman* by Renoir (1917) and, in the pond, *The Fountain* by Jean Tinguely (1968).

Waag   1C3

In the centre of Nieuwmarkt square stands the 15th-century Weigh House. An interesting, seven-turreted building, its circular interior has a surprising number of niches and nooks. It housed the Amsterdam Historical Museum (p. 46) from 1926 until 1960 when the collection moved to Kalverstraat. The Waag now houses the Jewish Historical Museum (p. 48), though that, too, will move in due course to the Synagogue complex on Mr. Visserplein.

Criminals were hanged in Nieuwmarkt in the 17th century and their bodies were used for experimentation by the surgeons' guild which convened in the Waag. The surgeons invited Rembrandt to record the scene and this resulted in his two famous works, both called *The Anatomy Lesson*, one of Dr. Tulp and the other of Dr. Deijman.

Waterlooplein   4J6

At the centre of what was Amsterdam's Jewish quarter, Waterlooplein was best known for its bustling flea market, established here at the end of the 19th century. Currently, work is in progress on a new town hall and opera house, so, while the market retains the name, the street traders have moved to nearby Valkenburgerstraat.

Zuiderkerkhof Gateway   2C3

Opposite De Pinto Huis in Sint Antoniesbreestraat. Made around 1612 by the Englishman, Nicholas Stone, who was the architect Hendrick de Keyser's son-in-law.

Montelbaanstoren

OUT OF AMSTERDAM

Amsterdam is the capital of a small country and most other Dutch cities and places of interest are within easy reach of the city — you can be in The Hague or Delft in three-quarters of an hour and Rotterdam is only an hour away. Map references (J6) refer to the map on pp. 82-3.

Aalsmeer   K8

(19km/12mi from Amsterdam) Site of the world's biggest year-round **flower auction**, held Mon.-Fri. each morning until 1100 at St Trowle Aalsmeerse Bloemenveiling Hall. Electric buttons rather than the auctioneer's hammer indicate buyer interest. The town is situated on the Westeinder lakes and the blooms arrive in long flat punts. One of the biggest floral events, the Bloemencorso, takes place here annually on the first Saturday in September.

Alkmaar   G8

(40km/25mi from Amsterdam) Most famous for its Friday morning **cheese market** which takes place April-Sept. 1000-1200 in front of the Waag (Weigh House) with its carillon chiming out Dutch folk tunes. Round cheeses are piled high on the cobbled square as traditional bidding — involving handslapping and ending in a handshake — takes place all around. After auction the cheese porters, clad in white and sporting hats lacquered blue, green, yellow or red to indicate which company of the guild they belong to, carry the cheeses in wooden cradles to the Weigh House for the bill at the end of it all.

Alkmaar received its charter in 1254 and the city retains an old-world atmosphere. Gabled houses line its canals. Holland's oldest pipe organ is housed in the Gothic church, **St Laurenskerk** (built 1470-1516), and the **City Museum** contains some interesting 17th-century paintings.

Alphen aan den Rijn   M7

(36km/23mi from Amsterdam) A small busy town noted for its **Avifauna Bird Sanctuary,** open Mar.-Oct., Mon.-Fri. from 0900, Sun. from 1300. Thousands of tropical birds and polar birds live here while ostriches and emus stroll the lawns. Floodlit at night.

Amersfoort   M13

(51km/32mi from Amsterdam) The second largest city in the province of Utrecht, Amersfoort is full of atmosphere. The town is surrounded by a double ring of moats dating from the Middle Ages. It is a fairytale sort of place where houses have been built on and into the immense city walls. There are four city gates, including the 13th-century *Koppelpoort*, the 14th-century *Kamperbinnenpoort* and the 15th-century *Waterpoort   Monnikendam*. Although everything nearby is modern, time has stood still in Amersfoort. Pupils at the Onze Lieve Vrouwe Church bell-ringing school create most of Holland's bell melodies. **St Pieters-en-Bloklands Gasthuis** contains 16th-century furniture and utensils. More of the town's past can be seen in the **Flehite Museum** on Westsingel. The architect, Jacob van Campen, is buried in St Joris Church.

Apeldoorn

(89km/56mi from Amsterdam) The Netherlands' largest garden city. The nearby palace of **Het Loo** is a royal residence. The main attraction in the vicinity is **Hoge Veluwe National Park,** some 57sq.km/22sq.mi of unspoiled, game-rich lake, forest and moorland. The famous **Kroller-Muller Museum,** housing a select collection of old and new masters, stands in the middle of the park.

Delft   N5

(58km/36mi from Amsterdam) A pretty picture-postcard town where stately trees line canals spanned by small white bridges. Water taxis run in summer but the town can also be explored on foot. Voldersgracht is one of the most picturesque canals, the Koornmarkt is one of the most stately, but Delft's oldest canal is **Oude Delft Canal** dating back to 1000. **Gemeenlandshuis** nearby is the oldest dwelling, once used by the Counts of Holland. The founder of the Netherlands, William of Orange (the Silent) is buried, with other members of Dutch royalty, in the **Nieuwe Kerk**. He lived, and in 1584 was murdered, in the 15th-century **Prinsenhof** which stands opposite the 13th-century **Oude Kerk** where several famous admirals are buried. The town hall on Grote Markt is built in Italian Renaissance style. The market square itself is the liveliest quarter of Delft and an annual floodlit parade takes place here at the end of August.

Fine old Delft tiles and early pottery are displayed in the museum **Huis Lambert van Meerten**. Modern, hand-painted Delftware is produced at **De Porceleyne Fles** and **Delftse Pauw**, two major factories which can be visited.

Doorn   N13

(59km/37mi from Amsterdam) Home, from 1920 to 1941, of the exiled emperor,

Wilhelm II, Kaiser of Germany. His house is now a museum containing many treasures from the former German royal house, including Frederick the Great's snuff boxes and fine Gobelin tapestries. The Kaiser's remains are entombed in the adjacent mausoleum.

Edam   H10
(22km/14mi from Amsterdam) Famous for its round red-skinned cheeses which are exported all over the world. A collection of cheese-making utensils is on view in the weigh house on the Kaasmarkt. But most of the historic sites are on the Damplein, including the magnificent, 18th-century, decorated **Town Hall** and the **Municipal Museum**, once a 17th-century sea captain's house. The 15th-century **Grote Kerk** contains some valuable stained glass, rare books and a 17th-century classroom complete with desks. Tallest landmark is the **Speeltoren** whose old carillon was cast in Malines (capital of the Netherlands from 1507-1530, now a city — also called Mechelen — in the north of Belgium).

Enkhuizen   F12
(62km/39mi from Amsterdam) A Zuider Zee port that once housed a 400-strong herring fleet and many more people than it does today. One of its main attractions is the open-air **Zuider Zee Museum** which shows the culture of the area. (In 1932 the Zuider Zee was sealed off from the North Sea by the Afsluitdijk dam, turned into a freshwater lake and renamed IJsselmeer.) One part of the museum has 130 houses along streets, canals and alleys, portraying life between 1880 and 1932. The other part, the Binnenmuseum, has a ship hall housing old sailing ships, traditional costumes and interiors plus a collection of model ships. The former is open daily, Apr.-Oct., 1000-1700, the latter is open Mon.-Sat., Feb.-Dec., 1000-1700; Sun. 1200-1700.

Enkhuizen has several museums of interest: the one in the 16th-century weigh house in the Kaasmarkt shows 17th-century medical equipment, the one in the 17th-century town hall in Breetstraat displays Gobelin tapestries and Paulus Potter paintings. Buildings of historic note include the double-towered **Dromedaris** fortification (1540) by the harbour front — the gateway has a beautiful carillon. **Herenhuis** is one of many handsome old houses lining the main street, Westerstraat, which runs east from the 17th-century Westerpoort gate. Inside, **Westerkerk** has fine wood vaulting, a 16th-century rood screen, organ, manuscripts and tapestries. The 15th-

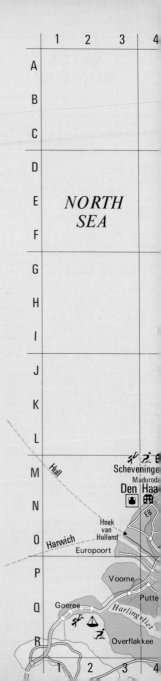

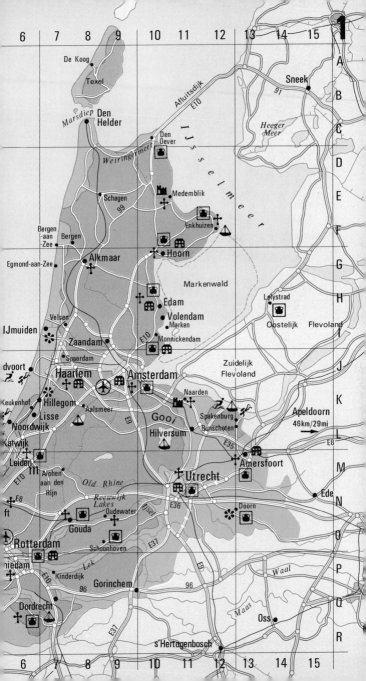

The cheese market in Alkmaar

The Koppelpoort in Amersfoort

The market place in Delft

The famous blue and white Delftware

Vredespaleis (Peace Palace) in The Hague

Advertising the newspaper Haagsche Courant

century **Zuiderkerk** has a 43-bell carillon and painted vaults.

Gouda   O7

(53km/33mi from Amsterdam) Most famous for its Thursday morning **Farmers' Cheese Market**, 0900-1200 from mid-May to mid-September, held in front of the ornate Weigh House. Painted farm wagons are used to transport the cheeses to the Weigh House. Inside the building you can sample some cheese, watch a film about cheese-making and see demonstrations of some of the local crafts. Gouda is also known for the manufacture of clay pipes — **De Moriaan Museum** in Westhave is devoted to them and they're still made in the Goedewaagen factory.

Catharina Gasthuis on Oosthave houses the Municipal Museum containing a collection of instruments of torture but also some fine paintings by Rubens, period rooms, plus unique objects such as Countess Jacqueline of Bavaria's 15th-century golden chalice. **Janskerk**, with the longest nave in the country, is said to have the finest stained-glass windows in the Netherlands — 64 of them, 14 of which are 16th-century Burgundian glass and some 12 accredited to Wouter and Dirk Crabeth. The windows portray such public figures of the time as William of Orange (the Silent) and Philip II of Spain. The church (15th-century) was rebuilt after a 16th-century fire.

Haarlem   J7

(23km/14mi from Amsterdam) Centre of the tulip trade, only 9km/6mi inland from the North Sea coast, Haarlem was where the painter Frans Hals was born in 1580. The **Frans Hals Museum**, at Groot Heiligland 62, is housed in one of the town's typical gabled almshouses dating from 1608. To tour the house by candlelight is memorable. In summer, Saturday evening music recitals are given here (also on some holiday weekends, such as Easter). Pride of the museum are the group portraits of governors and militia, including two which Hals painted when he was aged 80. But there are also Haarlem landscapes and period rooms, an 18th-century dolls' house and old printing equipment.

Other museums of interest include the **Teylers** with a collection of old prints and an odd assortment of inventions; **Croquus**, a former steam-pumping station close to the Heemstede, demonstrating land reclamation techniques; and **Visschoppelijk**, on Janenstraat, with an excellent collection of ecclesiastical paintings and porcelain.

Founded in the 10th century, Haarlem has been besieged, stormed and devastated in its time, but what makes it unique is its core, a beautifully preserved 700-year-old city heart in which the Middle Ages loom over the modernity of the 20th century. Grote Markt, for example, was once a jousting arena. Bordering it is the 15th-century church of **St Bavo** whose cross-vaulted cedar roof is supported inside by 28 columns. Mozart and Handel played the organ in this church and Frans Hals is buried here. The **Town Hall**, part of which used to be the hunting lodge of a medieval count, has a candlelit and tapestried council chamber. Then there is the **Vleeshal** (meat market), a fine Renaissance building which is today an exhibition hall, and the **Vishal**, an 18th-century fish hall.

To the north stretches the garden suburb of **Bloemendaal**. As an additional reminder that Haarlem is surrounded by bulbfields, every spring 20 local belles are chosen to greet visitors with a 'welcome' flower.

The Hague   N4

(60km/38mi from Amsterdam) The seat of government of the Netherlands, The Hague (Den Haag) is a stately city of imposing buildings and much greenery. Technically, it is still a village since Count Floris never actually gave it a city charter, but it is everything a diplomatic city and the seat of government should be. There are three royal palaces, innumerable parks, the Knights' Hall, ministeries, embassies and diplomatic offices.

Chief attraction is the **Binnenhof** (Inner Court), originally a hunting lodge that grew to encompass parliament. It is surrounded by museums, elegant town houses and shopping centres. Some of the Binnenhof's walls and arches date from the 13th century when it was William II's residence. At the heart of the Binnenhof is the **Ridderzaal** (Knights' Hall), the magnificent Gothic building in which the Dutch parliament meets. On the third Tuesday in September, the Queen arrives in an open, golden, horse-drawn carriage to open parliament here. It is reached through the 17th-century Grenadierspoort.

There are some 22 museums in The Hague and none finer than **Mauritshuis**, next door to the parliament buildings. It was built for a 17th-century court dandy by Pieter Post between 1633 and 1644, and was Holland's first Italian Renaissance-style structure. Many of the paintings on view today were original furnishings of the palace but it is the royal picture collection (moved here in 1821) which forms the museum's nucleus. It houses Rembrandt's *The Anatomy Lesson of Dr.*

Tulp, Vermeer's *View of Delft* and many other fine old masters.

The **Gemeentemuseum**, or Municipal Museum, contains the world's largest collection of paintings by Mondriaan, noted for his abstract works. The 154 paintings were bequeathed by an estate agent who had befriended Piet Mondriaan at the time when he was still painting Dutch landscapes. There are also works here by Monet, Picasso and Braque and sculptures by Rodin, Degas and Moore. The museum also contains an unusual collection of musical instruments and manuscripts, plus numerous superb dolls' houses.

The **Nederlands Postmuseum** (Dutch Postal Museum), at Zeestraat 82, is concerned with various forms of communication, not just mail. Exhibits include the world's first radio station. The **Bredius Museum**, Prinsengracht 6, was the home of Mijnheer Bredius. Old masters, fine porcelain and silver are displayed here. Another town house is now the **Mesdag Museum** at Laan van Meerdervoort 7. It was owned by a burgher who helped to found The Hague School of painting. There are good examples of works by Corot, Courbet and Rousseau among others here. Not only a collector, Mesdag was also a painter, and his **Panorama Mesdag**, on view at Zeestraat 65b, is probably the most popular museum in The Hague. It came about when the city authorities in Scheveningen (The Hague's coastal neighbour) decided to re-landscape the sand dunes. By way of protest, Mesdag and other local painters created this huge panorama of the seafront as it was in 1881 on a canvas 14m/45ft high and 122m/400ft in circumference.

Until 1828 the **Gevangenpoort** was a prison (Holland's oldest). Now it has become the Prison Gate Museum containing instruments of torture in a particularly comprehensive collection. It is located at Buitenhof 33 (across the street from the Binnenhof). Near the museum is the statue of Johan de Witt, a former prisoner in the Gevangenpoort.

The **Vredespaleis** (Peace Palace), on Carnegieplein, is where the International Court of Justice sits. The site is named after the Scottish-American steel millionaire, Andrew Carnegie, who contributed $1.5 million towards its construction. It is built in Flamboyant Flemish style from a plan submitted by Louis Cordonnier of Lille, and it contains elaborate decorations donated by several countries. The lobby's floor and pillars, for example, are of Italian marble and the porcelain fountain is from Denmark. There is also a three-ton jasper vase contributed by Czar Nicholas II.

The Hague's Gothic **Town Hall** (1564) is in Gravenstraat near the **Church of St Jacob** (14th-century) where you can see a fine 15th-century pulpit and the arms of the Knights of the Golden Fleece. Only a short distance east of the city centre, on the far side of the Haagse Bos (Hague Woods), is the **Huis ten Bosch**, residence of the royal family.

Hilversum   L11

(34km/21mi from Amsterdam) A strikingly modern city, perfectly planned by W.M. Dudok with wide tree-lined streets, pedestrian precincts, and a town hall that resembles a luxury hotel. It is Holland's broadcasting centre but it is also so clean and wreathed in flowers that it is often called the 'garden of Amsterdam'.

Hook of Holland   O3

(80km/50mi from Amsterdam) A port at the mouth of the waterway from Rotterdam, of interest to all shipping buffs.

Keukenhof   K6

(34km/21mi from Amsterdam) Holland's most famous **flower garden** situated in the small town of Lisse. Its 28-hectare/70-acre spread is open from 0800 to sunset from about 1 April to mid-May, depending upon the weather (the tulip season can be later). There are lakes, greenhouses, sculpture gardens and a windmill here, but it is the sight of thousands of flowers of all shades, in full bloom, that is so overwhelming.

Kinderdijk   P7

(110km/69mi from Amsterdam) Noted for its **windmills**, this area in the Alblasserwaard district, lies halfway between Rotterdam and Dordrecht where the rivers Nieuwe Maas, Lek and Noord meet. There are 19 windmills in operation here — you can see them all in motion every Saturday afternoon during July and August. From April to September, at least one of the mills is in operation every day and can be inspected. Inside there are concealed closet beds and a stove. This area began to be reclaimed in the 10th century. Many streams and rivers run through it and the houses are built on top of dykes for flood protection.

Leiden   M6

(40km/25mi from Amsterdam) Holland's oldest university town, Leiden was already an important settlement in 800 and, in the 14th century, a great weaving centre. Besieged by Spain in 1574, the town held out for a year against all odds and was finally saved by William the Silent who ordered the dykes to be cut so that the

Windmill in Kinderdijk (inset)

'n Keukenhof garden

Dutch could sail to the rescue over the flooded land. Relief boats brought bread and herring to the starving city and now, every 3 October, Leiden celebrates the memory of this event by handing out loaves and herring to everyone. To thank the citizens for their bravery under siege, William offered a tax remission or a university. The citizens chose the latter, and the univesity was founded in 1575. It had become a famous European teaching centre by the 17th century.

The historic centre of the old town is the **Burcht**, a 12th-century, artificial mound with a fortress on top. Around this focal point a maze of narrow streets and alleys twist and turn, crossing the many canals. Across the Rapenburg canal stands **Leiden University**. The main building, the 16th-century Academie, was once a nunnery and now houses a museum; the **Botanical Gardens** behind the university also date from the 16th century. Take Nieuwestraat to reach the 15th-century **Hooglandsekerk** with little houses along its walls and, inside, the tomb of van der Werff (burgomaster during the Spanish siege). The city's greatest church, **St Pieterskerk**, reached via the Papengracht, took 300 years to build. A plaque commemorates the Pilgrim Fathers and their pastor, John Robinson, who is buried, along with the painter Jan Steen, in the church.

Mementoes of the Pilgrims are scattered throughout the town. The Puritans fled from England to Leiden where they were accepted before eventually heading for the New World, in 1620. Items connected with their 11-year stay in the town are on show in the **Pilgrim Fathers' House**, at Boisotkade 2a. Other historic buildings to see include the **Gravensteen** prison (13th-17th centuries) and the 17th-century **Town Hall** (damaged by fire in 1929 but partially restored) on the main thoroughfare of Breestraat.

Lakenhal Museum, on Oude Singel 28, was built originally as a Cloth Hall (the guildhall of the cloth weavers) in 1639. It contains exhibits relating to the town's history as well as housing important works of art. Many of the latter are by local citizens such as Rembrandt (who was born here in 1606), Lucas van Leyden and Jan van Goyen. Other museums worth seeing include **Rijksmuseum van Oudheden**, at Rapenburg 28, for its collection of Egyptian, Roman, Greek and prehistoric items, the **Ethnological Museum** with its Buddha Room and the **Science Museum**. The unusual **De Valk Windmill Museum** is an eight-storey windmill, one of 19 flour mills which once lined the city walls.

Madurodam   M4

(60km/38mi from Amsterdam) Haringkade 175, on one side of a canal connecting The Hague to Scheveningen. This is Holland in miniature. Madurodam is a toy town, at a scale of 1:25, showing many cities and buildings in meticulous detail. The models include a harbour with light house, quayside with ferries, airport trains, amusement parks and windmills. What makes it special is that everything works — traffic moves along four-lane highways, mill sails turn and the light house flashes its signals. When the sun sets, all the lights go on in the houses, streets are lit and castles floodlit.

Holland in miniature at Madurodam

Marken   I10

(22km/14mi from Amsterdam) A village notable for its costumed inhabitants. Once an island, Marken was built on stilts because of the danger of flooding. It is still almost entirely surrounded by water but today a dyke road connects it to the mainland. The local costume is widely worn and comprises: for the women, red and white bodices covered with bright sleeveless fronts, dark skirts and an embroidered lace cap sometimes held in place by a ribbon. The costume worn by men is blue blouses and baggy linen knee breeches under red belts. Traditionally, children under five are dressed alike — in skirts, though boys' skirts are blue.

Monnickendam   I10

(15km/9mi from Amsterdam) A pretty little town with a history dating back to 1355 when it acquired its city charter. Because of its easy access to Amsterdam, the East India trade brought the town 17th-century riches. Look for the 18th-century **Town Hall** and the **Speeltoren** (16th-century bell tower) whose carillon sets a procession of knights in motion when the hour chimes. On the waterfront stands an old **Waag**, or weigh house, and the **Museum Stuttenburgh** contains music boxes and mechanical musical instruments.

Naarden   K11

(21km/13mi from Amsterdam) Holland's best-preserved fortress town, built in 1350 to defend an expanding Amsterdam. It was captured in 1572 by Don Frederick of Toledo who massacred most of the inhabitants. The main visitor attraction is the **Grote Kerk** whose fine acoustics make a trip to hear Bach's *St Matthew Passion* on Good Friday most rewarding.

Noordwijk aan Zee   L5

(40km/25mi from Amsterdam) A beach resort in the flower-growing district west of Lisse. The main street, Koningin Wilhelmina Boulevard, runs right along the beachfront and is lined with hotels, cafés and restaurants. All the amenities you might expect of an international seaside resort are to be found in Noordwijk — good shops, children's amusements and sporting activities from sailing, swimming and waterskiing to bowling, tennis and horse riding. The town's modern arcaded square has fountains, seats and shops and is overlooked by a lighthouse.

Rotterdam   O6

(76km/48mi from Amsterdam) Holland's second city is situated on the estuaries of the Maas (Meuse) and the Rhine. Although it is actually 32km/20mi inland, it is also the world's largest seaport and one of Europe's main trading centres, earning it the title of 'Europoort'. An ultramodern city (rebuilt after World War II), Rotterdam has many smart shops and restaurants and pedestrian precincts such as the **Lijnbaan**, ornamented with flowers and statues. There are no canals and few old houses, though the town hall did withstand the bombings. Today's landmark is the **Euromast** overlooking the city from a height of some 183m/600ft. There is a platform at 31m/102ft and, at 91m/300ft, a bar, coffee shop and restaurant. The revolving space tower takes visitors up to the top of the Euromast where the view extends for 50km/32mi all round on a clear day.

Boymans-van Beuningen Museum, Mathenesserlaan 18-20, contains masterpieces from many schools of art and includes paintings by Hals, Steen, Monet and Brueghel. There is also a fine collection of porcelain, glass and silver. The **Museum of Ethnology**, Willemskade 25, and **Professor van der Poel**

Rotterdam port seen from the Euromast

Tax Museum, Parklaan 14-16, are two others for rainy-day enjoyment.

Tucked into Rotterdam's maze of docks is **Delfshaven**, a timeless district where 16th-century houses are mirrored in a quiet lagoon. Much favoured by artists, Delfshaven used to be a town in its own right and it was from the harbour here that the Pilgrim Fathers set sail for America in 1620.

Some of the old houses have been restored and converted into antique shops and art galleries. The **Zakkendragershuisje** (Guild House of the Grain Sack Carriers), at Voorstraat 13-15, is now a group of workshops where craftsmen demonstrate their skills.

Scheveningen   M4

(60km/38mi from Amsterdam) A bright cosmopolitan beach resort on The Hague's doorstep. The restored **Kurhaus** is now a hotel boasting a large casino offering roulette and black jack at 24 tables. The glass-enclosed recreational centre, Wave Pool, features swimming pools, a whirlpool, saunas, solariums and sports rooms.

Scheveningen is particularly lively in summer when there are art exhibitions, firework displays, etc., but there are plenty of restaurants, shops and amusements to suit all ages and budgets at any time of year. Much of the action takes place around the pier which links four artificial 'islands', combining a fun park with shopping arcade, bars and a lookout tower.

Utrecht   M11

(35km/22mi from Amsterdam) Capital of the province of Utrecht and Holland's fourth largest city. It has been a Roman fortress, a Franconian citadel and a

In Volendam

church mission station. The War of Spanish Succession was ended by the Treaty of Utrecht signed, in 1579, in the university chapter hall. Today the city is a very modern, commercial centre.

Its old quarter, however, is still dominated by the **Dom** cathedral on Domplein. Construction began in 1254 and it took 300 years to complete. The tower, open May-Sept., has 465 steps but the view from the top is worth the climb. The main shopping streets are located between the cathedral and Vreedenburg Square, beside the Hoog Catharijne shopping precinct, but there are also interesting streets around Oude Gracht. (The old quarter is full of small streets and delightful canals.)

There are several Roman and Gothic churches worth visiting: **St Pieterskerk**, behind the cathedral, is interesting for its frescoes and unusual crypt, and the **Paushuis** (1523) on Kromme Nieuwe Gracht, commemorates Holland's only Pope, Adrian VI. You'll also find old *hofjes* (almshouses) and patrician houses such as **Bartholomeus Gasthuis**, in Lange Smeestraat, which contains magnificent Gobelin tapestries, while **Het Catharijne convent** (St Catherine's Convent) gives the history of Dutch Christianity from the 8th to the 20th centuries.

Among the museums, look in on the **Music Box and Barrel Organ Museum**, Achter de Dom 12 — a wonderland of flute clocks, barrel organs and musical snuffboxes. Some are strictly decorative, some commercial, and some extremely complex. The **Centraal Museum**, Agnietenstraat 1, contains paintings, furnishings, pottery and costumes. For railway buffs, the **Railway Museum**, Johan van Oldebarneveltlaan 6, shouldn't be missed.

Volendam   I10
(20km/12.5mi from Amsterdam) A fishing village noted for its colourful local costumes, it is often combined with a sightseeing trip of Marken. Here, the men's costume comprises baggy black trousers, long sleeveless waistcoats fastened with silver buttons, and round black caps. Women wear winged lace bonnets and long striped skirts.

Zandvoort   J6
(29km/18mi from Amsterdam) A swinging beach resort much favoured by Amsterdammers. Destroyed completely in World War II, it has been rebuilt in modern splendour with many hotels and shops, cabarets and amusements. The promenade stretches for 3km/2mi and sporting activities include an 18-hole golf course, motor-racing circuit, plus open-air swimming pools. There are plenty of sites for campers and wooded dunes for those who enjoy walking.

INDEX

All place names, buildings and monuments which have a main entry are printed in heavy type. Map references also appear in heavy type and refer to Amsterdam City Maps between pp. 33–45.